MARCO  POLO

SCOTLAND

with Local Tips
*The author's special recommendations are
highlighted in yellow throughout this guide*

P9-CRF-132

There are five symbols to help you find your way around this guide:

Marco Polo's top recommendations – the best in each category

sites with a scenic view

where the local people meet

where young people get together

(102/A1)
pages and coordinates for the road atlas
(U/A1) *coordinates for the city map of Edinburgh inside back flap*
(O) *outside area covered by the city map*

MARCO ⊕ POLO

Travel guides and language guides in this series:

Algarve • Amsterdam • Australia • Berlin • Brittany • California
Channel Islands • Costa Brava/Barcelona • Costa del Sol/Granada
Côte d'Azur • Crete • Cuba • Cyprus • Eastern USA • Florence • Florida
Gran Canaria • Greek Islands/Aegean • Ibiza • Ireland • Istanbul • Lanzarote
London • Mallorca • Malta • New York • New Zealand • Normandy • Paris
Prague • Rhodes • Rome • Scotland • South Africa • Southwestern USA
Tenerife • Turkish Coast • Tuscany • Venice • Western Canada

French • German • Italian • Spanish

*Marco Polo would be very interested to hear your
comments and suggestions. Please write to:*

North America:
Marco Polo North America
70 Bloor Street East
Oshawa, Ontario, Canada
(B) 905-436-2525

United Kingdom:
World Leisure Marketing Ltd
Marco Polo Guides
Newmarket Drive
Derby DE24 8NW

*Our authors have done their research very carefully, but should any errors or omissions
have occurred, the publisher cannot be held responsible for any injury, damage
or inconvenience suffered due to incorrect information in this guide*

Cover photograph: Piper by Loch Lomond (Mauritius: Nägele)
*Photographs: Amberg (37); Lade: BAV (26), Krecichwost (77), Thompson (48);
Mauritius: Hubatka (101), Keane (54), Löhr (22), Mehlig (19), Nägele (14), Photo Bank (30),
Thonig (4, 6, 7, 9, 46, 62, 70), Torino (72), Vidler (16); Santor (24, 36); Schapowalow: Brooke
(45, 68, 82), Heaton (10, 51, 59), Messerschmid (40), Nebe (84); Nebbia (20);
Schuster: Explorer (15), Ikeda (56), Kasch (66); Transglobe: Deterding (80, 86),
Krecichwost (23), Wegg (32)*

2nd revised edition 1999
© Mairs Geographischer Verlag, Ostfildern, Germany
Author: Axel Patitz
Translation: Paul Fletcher
English edition 1999: Gaia Text
Editorial director: Ferdinand Ranft
Chief editor: Marion Zorn
Cartography Road Atlas: © Mairs Geographischer Verlag
Design and layout: Thienhaus/Wippermann
Printed in Germany

CONTENTS

Discover Scotland

Highlands and Lowlands, bens and glens –
from the Borders to the Orkneys, Scotland's wild
landscape offers infinite variety

Scotland's identity is universally linked with whisky, kilts and bagpipes, romantic lochs and desolate hills smothered in purple heather, but its many qualities extend far beyond these common clichés. It is, of course, a country of outstanding natural beauty where the past is still very much alive. But far from being locked in tradition, it is a forward-thinking country, currently in the process of great change.

If you are approaching Scotland from south of the border, the minute you pass the roadside 'Scotland' sign and leave northern England behind, you begin to sense that you are venturing into a whole new world. This is especially true if, instead of following the A1 coast road, you take the inland approach on the A68 which goes through the Borders. Stretching away in all directions to the horizon are the rolling Cheviot Hills – as lonely and as tranquil as the bare, gently sloping

Loch Affric in the autumn, when the Scottish countryside takes on a warm golden hue

bens (peaks) of the Highland mountains in the north. Sparsely populated, inhabited largely by the thick-fleeced Cheviot sheep, and with no marshland or stony screes for miles around, this is ideal walking and riding country.

When the Romans conquered Britain, they found they were no match for the fierce, warlike Picts and Scots who inhabited the north. Hadrian's Wall was built in AD 120-123 to keep the hostile northern tribes out of Roman territory, however it also stopped the invaders from discovering the idyllic landscape that lay beyond the Cheviot Hills. Today, the Borders region is often overlooked by tourists beating a path to the Highlands, but it is a part of the country that definitely merits exploration. Here, in the green hills of the Tweed and Teviot valleys, lie the small towns of Kelso, Dryburgh and Melrose with their romantic ruins of abbeys and castles. The beauty and peace of these sites belies their bloody history. The Borders was under constant attack from the English and it was not for purely religious reasons that so many great abbeys were

Abbotsford House, the home of Sir Walter Scott

built here. The Scottish kings invited the Augustinian and Cistercian monks to settle the area to form a line of defence against invaders. The Scots have always held these grand old ruins close to their hearts. They buried the heart of Robert the Bruce, their greatest king, under the high altar of Melrose Abbey, while the remains of the great 19th-century writer, Sir Walter Scott, lie in the majestic ruins of Dryburgh. If you visit Melrose Abbey, you should also take a look at Abbotsford House on the River Tweed. It was built by Scott and is still lived in by his descendants today. It was here that he wrote so many of his works, drawn from real events in Scotland's turbulent history. It was Scott, in fact, who first painted the romantic picture of Scotland with which we are so familiar today.

Over and above Sir Walter Scott, Scotland's greatest literary figure is the poet Robert Burns. The birthplace of the Scottish bard lies further west, beyond the border town of Gretna Green. Robert Burns was born in 1759 in Alloway, near Ayr on the southwest coast. 'Rabbie', as he is affectionately known, came into the world in a dismal, windowless cottage and brought up his 15 children in poverty. But despite, or even because of his humble background, Burns helped restore the Scots' self-esteem and became a national hero. Ironically, neither he nor Scott were Highlanders. They were Lowland Scots from the south, where the inhabitants have more in common with their English neighbours than with their Celtic countrymen to the north. The differences between Lowlanders and Highlanders still remain strong and inform everything from the local culture to language and traditions.

The green and rural Borders country is not typical of the whole of the south. In Galloway, also known as 'Burns' Country', the landscape of the Forest Park around Loch Trool is surprisingly similar to the Highlands. Beyond it is the low-lying region between the River Clyde and the Firth of Forth where the main cities lie.

Edinburgh ranks as one of the world's finest cities. Although the weather is all too often damp, windy and bitterly cold, Scotland's capital will revive your heart and soul. The tenements, squares and narrow lanes of the

Old Town contrast with the broad streets and elegant buildings of the New Town. A stroll down the Royal Mile, the stretch of road that runs between the castle and Holyrood Palace, is like a journey back in time. This was where witches were once burned and public executions performed, where royal parades and sombre processions passed on their way to the castle. In the castle itself, you can view the room where Mary Queen of Scots gave birth to her son, who became James VI and I. At the time, many believed that the boy was not her son at all. Rumour had it that the real James had been murdered at birth and replaced by the child of a nurse. The truth was never disclosed, but in 1830, a fire in the royal chambers brought to light a small wooden coffin containing the bones and swaddling clothes of a child. Much of Edinburgh's appeal lies in its rich history and the mysteries and legends that surround it.

West of Edinburgh, and larger than its rival on the east coast, lies the vibrant city of Glasgow. While it has more than its fair share of social problems, in the last two decades this industrial metropolis has undergone a cultural renaissance. Much still remains to be done to undo years of economic decline, but the city is slowly recovering its pride. In 1990 Glasgow was deservedly voted 'European City of Culture'.

Beyond the cities begin the Highlands – the landscape most associated with Scotland. On the horizon loom the mighty bens, their colour changing with the seasons. The colour of the lochs also changes with the weather, from steel blue to inky black. The clouds, rain and wind are an integral part of the landscape; nowhere else does the weather affect the scenery so dramatically. When it rains here, it pours. Gale-force winds blast through the rocks, whipping up the water in the lochs and bays while the mist

Eilean Donan Castle in Loch Duich has been restored to its former splendour

History at a glance

3000–1500 BC
Orkney and Shetland Islands inhabited

500 BC
Scotland settled by Celts

5th century
Picts and Scots found kingdoms

6–7th century
Christianization of Scotland

843
Picts and Scots unified under Kenneth MacAlpine

11–12th century
Dispute over succession. Scotland ruled by English governor

13th century
William Wallace unites the Scots against the English

1328
England recognizes Scottish independence under Robert the Bruce

1371
The Stewart (later Stuart) dynasty takes power

1468
Denmark cedes Orkney and Shetland Islands to Scotland

1542
Birth of Mary Queen of Scots

1542-60
Reformation splits the country. Calvinist John Knox founds the Presbyterian Church, which becomes the national church

1567
Mary Queen of Scots abdicates. She is executed in 1587

1603
Elizabeth I dies childless. James VI, king of Scotland and son of Mary Queen of Scots, becomes king of England as James I

1688–89
End of the Stuart dynasty. The crown of James VII and II is given to William and Mary

1707
Union with England

1745–46
Bonnie Prince Charlie claims the Scottish throne. His army is routed at the Battle of Culloden

1750–1850
Highland Clearances

1850–1950
Period of economic prosperity. Glasgow shipyards work full tilt

1968
Oil found in the North Sea. Scottish autonomy becomes an important issue

1979
Scots vote on devolution, but do not reach a big enough majority

1993
Braer oil tanker disaster off the Shetland Islands

1997
Labour wins General Election and pledges to give Scotland greater autonomy. In a referendum in September, Scots vote decisively in favour of devolution

1999
First elections for a Scottish national assembly

closes in. But within minutes, the wind can drop, the clouds disperse and the sun emerge.

To enjoy wild and windblown Scotland, head for the west coast where you can hide away in remote bays and walk across hundreds of acres of Highland hillside without meeting a soul. The Inner and Outer Hebrides attract visitors in search of solitude. Skye, the biggest of the islands, can now be reached via a bridge. Mountaineers come from all over the world to the Cuillins, a range of basalt peaks rising up to 1000 m (3300 ft) from the island's unspoilt moorland. From the dramatic cliffs along the coast you can look across to the neighbouring islands of Rona and Raasay. The remote Outer Hebrides, the Orkney and Shetland Islands stubbornly resist the winds and waves of the Atlantic that batter their rocky coasts. Remains of ancient cultures testify to the islands' long history, although they only came under Scottish rule in 1468, when the King of Denmark relinquished control. However, the people did not give up their Viking customs and language easily. The dialect spoken by the fishermen in Lerwick harbour still includes many Norse words.

One of Scotland's most important historic sites is Culloden, near Inverness. It was here, in 1746, that the Duke of Cumberland routed the clans led by Bonnie Prince Charlie, quashing the Scots' last hopes for independence. Soon afterwards the Clearances began, sealing the fate of the Highlands. Under the Clearances Act, landlords evicted tenants to turn their farms into grazing land for sheep. Many crofters were forced to emigrate to America, Canada, New Zealand and Australia. Today, only 4% of Scotland's 5 million inhabitants live in the Highlands.

As you travel through the Highlands and Lowlands, passing historic castles and the sites of Jacobite uprisings, you may well reflect on the links between past and present. With the impending change in Scotland's constitution arising from the 1997 referendum, the relevance of Scottish history will be high on the agenda for some time to come.

The Standing Stones of Callanish on the island of Lewis

Customs and culture

Scotland's Celtic past continues to influence the present

Architecture

The predecessor of the Scottish castle was the broch (Pictish tower) which dates back to the 1st century AD. The best preserved of the 400 or so ruins can be seen on the Shetland island of Mousa. By the 14th century, the defensive dwelling had evolved into the 'tower house' – a tall and narrow castle with thick walls (eg Threave Castle, Castle Fraser and Crathes Castle). After the Reformation, which brought new wealth to the gentry, more decorative elements were added to the tower house and it was expanded with wings into an L- or Z-shaped form. The tower house form reached its peak in the Scottish Baronial style of the late 16th and early 17th century. In the 18th and 19th century, this style took on a more romantic form. The finest examples of neo-Baronial architecture are Abbotsford House and Balmoral. The Georgian style of the early 18th century was characterized by symmetry and clear lines (Duff House, Hopetoun House). One of the best-known exponents of this style was William Adam. His son, Robert Adam (1728-1792),

finished Hopetoun House, begun by his father, and became one of the most famous architects of his time. The best example of his work is Culzean Castle. The most influential Scottish architect and designer of the early 20th century was Charles Rennie Mackintosh (1868-1928), who became the main exponent of the Art Nouveau movement in Scotland (Glasgow School of Art, Willow Tea Rooms).

Clans

The word 'clan' comes from the Gaelic *clann* which actually means 'children'. The Highland clans formed a distinct social unit. Every clan member bore the name of the head of the family or chief (Mac means 'son of') who was their ruler. In return for his leadership and protection, the members pledged him their allegiance. Each clan had its own justice system and, of course, its own tartan with the traditional checked pattern and colours. Distantly related tribes, known as septs, came under the command of the larger clans. Sovereignty over the various tribal regions had no legal basis and the territories were not clearly marked, which led to bloody struggles between rival clans. Although the boundaries of these

A pipe band playing outside Edinburgh Castle

regions were often disputed, they nevertheless remained largely unchanged over the centuries.

The clan system was still strong in 1707, when the Treaty of the Union united the parliament of Scotland with that of England. When Bonnie Prince Charlie was defeated at the Battle of Culloden in 1746, many of the clansmen who had backed him were executed or transported. Then in 1747 the Act of Proscription was passed, which banned Highland dress and the bearing of arms. These repressive laws, coupled with the Highland Clearances, destroyed the clans' power bases and resulted in their eventual disintegration.

Today there are approximately 100 clans still in existence. There are a number of clan societies in Scotland and abroad who are active in the upkeep of museums and ancestral seats.

Clearances

The northern Highlands is a sparsely populated region. Although the soil is not very fertile and the terrain is rather bleak and inhospitable, at one time this part of Scotland supported a thriving farming community. Traces of settlements are still visible in the form of crumbling walls and other agricultural remnants scattered across the treeless landscape of a once cultivated land.

Following the Jacobite uprisings that culminated in the Battle of Culloden, English anger at Scottish rebelliousness finally reached a peak. The government acted to suppress the clans and claimed their territories for the Crown. The land was then sold to wealthy Englishmen and Lowland Scots, many of whom were lured down to London by the attractions of high society life and the desire to become part of the moneyed elite. Life was expensive in the capital and in order to finance their extravagant lifestyles, the ruthless landlords charged exorbitant rents that the clan chiefs could ill afford. In the first half of the last century, the Highlands and islands saw the cruel eviction of defenceless crofters and peasants by the all-powerful landlords. The aim of the Clearances was to remove the crofters and turn the land over to pasture for sheep, as wool was much more profitable and southern sheep-farmers needed more land for their animals. As a result, many of the already impoverished owners of the smallholdings were forced to emigrate either to America, Canada, Australia or New Zealand. George Levenson-Gower, a wealthy industrialist who married into the Sutherland family and who was later ennobled by the English king, was regarded as one of the most ruthless of the Highland landlords.

Today, with only 2.6 inhabitants per sq km, the north-west of Scotland is one of the most thinly populated regions in Europe.

Devolution

Ever since the Act of Union in 1707, political groupings have sought to sever links with London and restore Scottish independence. Their voices were largely unheard until the 1960s, when the Scottish National Party (SNP) began to gain prominence on the political stage. In 1967 Winnie Ewing won a by-election in Hamilton and by the end of 1974 the SNP had 11 MPs, having won 30% of the total Scots vote. The SNP's agenda was independence from London. Their campaigns focused on such issues as the minimal benefits of North Sea oil for the Scottish people and they exploited the commonly held view that London ignored the wishes of the Scots. In 1979 the Labour government, dependent on SNP MPs in parliament and generally sympathetic to the transfer of some power from London to Edinburgh, gave the Scots the opportunity to express their views. Although 33% of Scots voted in favour of the proposals for devolved government in the referendum, 40% was the required figure and the plans collapsed.

The subject of devolution lost much of its potency when the Conservatives were elected that year. Margaret Thatcher argued that devolution would lead to the breakup of the United Kingdom and that was not what the Scots wanted.

Nevertheless, the SNP, Labour and the Liberal Democrats continued to argue for varying degrees of independence for Scotland. Their case was strengthened when the Conservative party introduced the Poll Tax, or Community Charge, in Scotland before England. Generally seen as an unfair tax, even in England, its introduction galvanized public opinion and led to the formation of the Scottish Constitution Convention, an alliance of Labour, Liberal Democrats, trade unions, the church and other Scottish organizations who saw the time for change had finally come.

Support for the Conservatives in Scotland suffered dramatically as a result of their rigid adherence to the Union. In the 1997 election, the Tories lost every Scottish seat. The Labour government kept its promise to the Scottish people and held a referendum in September of the same year. New proposals, including plans for the new assembly to have tax-varying powers, received strong support and everything is going ahead for the election of the 129 new MSPs in May 1999. A site near Holyrood Palace in Edinburgh has been agreed on for the new parliament building.

Economy

Whisky is Scotland's main export and tourism the main industry. In 1968 oil and gas were discovered in the North Sea off the Scottish coast with reserves estimated at 3000 million tonnes. The North Sea oil boom brought new jobs to an otherwise depressed area and now around 50,000 people work in the industry.

Fishing also plays an important role in Scotland's economy. Aberdeen is the largest fishing port with an annual turnover of about 160,000 tonnes, followed by Ullapool, where about 80,000 tonnes of fish are landed each year.

Around 50 million sheep supply the raw material for the important wool industry. Thanks to modern management techniques and innovative designs, Scottish wool products are well known and sold throughout the world.

Flora and fauna

Owing to the warm Gulf Stream, the western coast of Scotland benefits from a mild climate. Surprisingly, some luxuriant, often exotic vegetation thrives here, including magnolias, eucalyptus trees, conifers and azaleas. In the spring and early summer, the broom and rhododendron burst into flower, painting a colourful picture. At higher altitudes, purple flowering heathers cover the otherwise barren moorland. For some time, a massive forestation programme has been underway and the face of northern Scotland has been slowly changing. The subtle brown tones are disappearing and being replaced by a monotone covering of pines. Recently, greater efforts have been made to maintain traditional ecosystems and to replant native trees like birches, oaks, alders, ash, hazel, whych elms and willows. In spring, the Outer Hebrides – South Uist in particular – are carpeted with beautiful wild flowers, orchids among them.

Scotland's wildlife is equally rich. It is estimated that as many as 250 pairs of golden eagles have made their home here – nowhere else in Europe is this fine species enjoying such a renaissance. After a period of extinction, the osprey has also returned. The northern Highlands and islands provide excellent habitats for bird life. The moors and bogs of Caithness and Sutherland support some unique species and are now considered rare habitats that need protection. Foula, Fetlar and Fair Isle, which belong to the Shetland group of islands, all have well-established bird sanctuaries. Here you may be able to hear the distinctive cry of the common corncrake, now almost extinct elsewhere in Britain, and see skuas, puffins and gannets. One of Scotland's most famous creatures is the grouse. The biggest of this family of game birds is the black-plumed capercaillie. Red and black grouse also thrive on the moors, though in recent years numbers have dwindled because it is hunted, and there is some concern about its future.

Rhododendrons in bloom beside Loch Etive near Oban

Shetland sheep

Mammals which thrive in Scotland include the pine marten, the wild cat, the wild goat, the beaver, the badger, the otter and the polecat, which is actually becoming a menace. Highland deer roam the hillsides in significant numbers. They are currently estimated at 350,000. Deer stalking is permitted but controlled.

Seals, dolphins, porpoises and whales can sometimes be spotted off the coast. The rivers and lochs are rich in fish, including perch, roach and the char, a rare Arctic fish from the ice age. Angling is another favourite outdoor activity. The Rivers Spey, Tweed, Tay and Dee are particularly renowned for salmon. Sea trout and rainbow trout are also sought-after prizes. Cod, mackerel and dogfish are plentiful in the offshore waters.

Golf

Generally recognized to be the birthplace of golf, Scotland boasts no less than 450 courses. The concentration of golf courses is higher here than in any other country in the world.

The origins of the game can be traced back to the Middle Ages. In 1457, King James III passed a law banning regular soldiers from playing the game. Historic documents in Perth's archives show that in 1503 James IV bought a new set of golf clubs from a bow-maker, and records found in Montrose indicate that in 1508 a golf club was cited as a murder weapon. The first recorded woman golfer was Mary Queen of Scots.

The Royal and Ancient Golf Club in St Andrews on the Fife peninsula is the headquarters of the game. Although it is by no means the oldest club in Scotland, it is here that the rules of the game are administered. The four 18-hole courses and the one 9-hole course for beginners are owned by the town council. If you are planning a golfing holiday, bear in mind that the courses get booked up in the peak months of July and August.

Highland Gatherings

Hammer-throwing, tossing the caber, tug-o-war, bagpipe and dancing competitions are the highlights of any Highland Gathering. These are colourful summer events where games of brute strength predominate. The games held at Braemar are the best known. Members of the royal family, on holiday at nearby Balmoral, always pay a visit to what is now a huge event. All the large towns organize their own Highland Gathering. They take place between June and September.

Jacobite Uprisings

The house of Stewart ruled Scotland from 1371 until 1688. When Elizabeth I died in 1603, her second cousin, James VI of Scotland, became James I of England and ruled both countries from London. In 1688 his son, James VII, was deposed from the British throne by his Protestant daughter, Mary, and her Dutch husband, William of Orange, who were crowned King and Queen. In 1707 Scotland was forced to accept the Union of Parliaments.

James VII fled to France where his son, James Edward Stuart had been raised. (Mary Queen of Scots, who had spent a long time in France, first adopted the French spelling of the name Stuart.) Many Scots remained loyal to the Stuarts and in 1715 and then again in 1722, the Old Pretender, as James Edward was known, gathered together a band of supporters and unsuccessfully tried to regain the throne. In 1745 his son, Charles Edward (admired for his boyish charm and commonly known as 'Bonnie Prince Charlie'), in turn made an attempt to reinstate himself as King of Scotland. Their supporters were known as Jacobites, from the Latin form of James, which is Jacobus.

Bonnie Prince Charlie landed at Glenfinnan on 19 August 1745, and gathered an army of 2000 loyal Highlanders. Enjoying some early successes in battle, he decided to set out with his small band of men for London, hoping that the English would rally to his cause. As a direct descendant of James VI of Scotland, he had claims to the English throne as well as the Scottish. By the time he had reached Derby, however, morale was low, so returned to Scotland. He was followed north by the English Duke of Cumberland, who faced him in battle at Drummossie Moor, near Cul-

The Highland Games: a splendid display of traditional costume and brute strength

loden, where Bonnie Prince Charlie's army was routed. The Jacobite captives and wounded were seen as traitors and were killed or transported without mercy. The Prince escaped to Europe with the help of a heroic young girl, Flora MacDonald. The failed uprising diminished all remaining hopes for a Stuart succession and for Scottish independence.

Kilts and tartans

The word 'kilt' is of Viking origin, while the word 'tartan' is originally Celtic. They both refer to the large pieces of cloth, also known as plaids, which the ancient Scots wore wrapped round their waists with a belt. Their vast, colourful, woollen plaids could be used in different ways, both for carrying things in and for providing excellent protection against the cold and damp climate. The modern kilt is a development of the plaid and only became fashionable at the beginning of the 18th century. The word tartan is now commonly used to refer to the checked pattern and colour schemes used on kilt material.

It is believed that the designs of the early plaids were related to the different clans and their territories. However, with the demise of the clans after the Battle of Culloden in 1746, the English conquerors passed the Act of Proscription which banned the wearing of tartans. Around 40 years later, the law was finally repealed, but by this time many of the traditional family colours and designs had already been lost. Only those which are depicted on old portraits can be regarded

as truly authentic. All the other clans had to have new patterns drawn up and a flood of new checks appeared throughout the Highlands.

During the ban, the Highland regiments had been exempt. They wore the Government or Black Watch tartan, introducing other colours to differentiate the regiments. It was they who made the kilt fashionable, together with George IV, who in 1822 appeared at Holyrood Palace in full Highland dress. As usual, the King set the fashion and the court scrambled to follow him, as did the rest of the country.

However, for those families who can trace their history back through many generations, the 1300 or so different tartans are more than just colourful fashion accessories. There may be several patterns linked to a certain family and the occasion will determine which pattern is worn. Each clan tartan is also divided up into groups. These include 'chief tartans' worn by the clan chiefs and their close relatives; 'military tartans' worn by the Scottish regiments; 'district tartans' for Scots who do not belong to any well-known clan; and 'royal tartans', which are reserved for members of the royal family.

To make a proper pleated kilt, up to 7 m of material are required. Only then will the tartan pattern be properly visible. The large blanket pin on the right-hand side is for decorative purposes only. Full traditional dress should include a waistcoat, either in tartan or black, knee-length woollen stockings, a sporran (a large pouch hung from the belt usually with a fur covering), a dagger (*skeandhu*) tucked into the right stocking, and neatly laced black shoes.

Language

Although it is feared that Scottish Gaelic is a dying language, in the Hebrides, Skye and the Western Highlands around 70,000 people still speak it on a daily basis. The islands of the Outer Hebrides are often referred to as the 'homelands of the Gael', as it is here that the traditional Gaelic lifestyle based around fishing, crofting and weaving still survives.

In the Grampian Highlands and Aberdeen the local dialect includes words of north European and sometimes French origin. Until 200 years ago, the everyday language spoken on the Orkney and Shetland Islands was similar to medieval Danish. The Shetlanders speak a mixture of Old Norse and English, interspersed with the odd Dutch and German word. Even in the rural regions of the Southern Lowlands, other English-speaking visitors may find the rich dialect difficult to understand at first.

Literature

The first heyday of Scottish literature began with the end of the Anglo-Scottish wars (1286-1342) in which William Wallace and Robert the Bruce played heroic roles. Famous works from this era include *The Bruce* (1375) by John Barbour, the first great Scottish poet, and *Wallace* (1461), said to be written by a blind singer by the name of Henry or Harry.

James MacPherson (1736-1796) has a special, if ignoble, place in Scottish literary history. He published the prose pieces *Fingal* and *Temora*, claiming that they were epic poems by the Gaelic bard, Ossian, which he had translated into English. Most of MacPherson's contribution turned out to be forged, as the two famous tales had never been written down in their full length.

Scotland's national poet and hero is Robert Burns (1759-96), who wrote in Scots dialect at a time when it was not considered suitably 'elevated' for literature. His most famous work is the narrative poem *Tam o' Shanter*. Burns' Night, held on his birthday, is still widely celebrated with a haggis supper and poetry recitals.

The historical novels and ballads of Sir Walter Scott (1771-1832) became famous during his lifetime. Classics such as *Lady of the Lake*, *Rob Roy* and *Ivanhoe* earned the writer fame beyond his country's borders.

Among the other great Scottish authors who have gained a worldwide readership are Sir Arthur Conan Doyle (1859-1930), creator of the legendary detective Sherlock Holmes, and Robert Louis Stevenson (1850-94), best known for the children's classic *Treasure Island* and the story of *Dr Jekyll and Mr Hyde*.

Military tattoo

The Edinburgh Military Tattoo is held every August on the Castle Esplanade. Music is performed by bands of pipers and drummers, all kitted out in full Scottish costume and regalia. A lone piper performs at the end of the ceremony.

Whisky

The Gaelic words *uisge beatha*, from which the word 'whisky' is derived, mean 'water of life'.

The giant stills in the distilleries hold untold volumes of the 'water of life'

Scots have been distilling whisky in the Highlands and islands for over 500 years. During the 18th century, known as the 'heroic age of whisky', much of the national drink was made in illicit stills as the government imposed a hefty tax on it. Not much has changed in the latter respect – in fact, taxation levels on whisky are proportionally higher nowadays. For every bottle of whisky sold, the Chancellor of the Exchequer takes about five times the actual cost of the spirit.

Most of the whisky distilleries are located on Speyside, and on the islands of Jura and Islay. Many of them run guided tours which usually last about an hour. You will be taken through the various stages of the process and your visit will be rounded off with a free 'dram'. The *Malt Whisky Trail* on Speyside is a 110-km voyage of discovery that takes in eight major distilleries.

The factors which make for a good malt whisky have been clearly established: clear spring water from snow melt; peat, over which the sprouting barley is kiln-dried; and a cool, damp climate for the storage period in oak and sherry barrels. Malt whisky is the primary product, while blended whisky is made up of about 20% malt whisky and the remainder of over a dozen different types of grain whisky. There are currently around three billion litres of whisky that have been maturing for up to twelve years or longer. Every year the equivalent of 160 million bottles of Scotch whisky are lost through evaporation.

Whisky lovers prefer specific brands, but it is ultimately a question of taste. Purists believe malt whisky must be drunk neat, or at most with a little water. They say any other addition spoils the taste. And remember – when in Scotland, never ask for Scotch!

Other popular whisky-based drinks include the liqueur Drambuie and Gingermac, also known as Whisky Mac – a warming mixture of whisky and ginger wine.

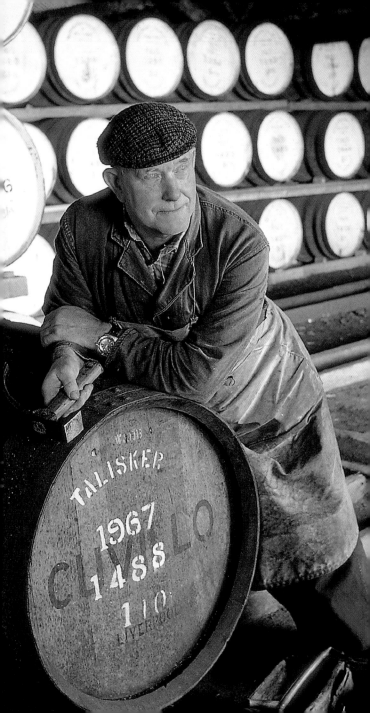

Arbroath Smokies and Cranachan

Scottish cooking benefits from an abundance of top quality local produce

Scotland is renowned for its natural produce and offers some of the best fish and seafood, meat and game in Europe. Haggis may be the national dish, but the list of other well-known Scottish favourites is long.

Given the chilly climate, hearty home-made soups are frequently served as a main dish for lunch or as a starter. Among the best known are Cock-a-Leekie, made with chicken and leeks; Scotch Broth, made with mutton stock, vegetables and barley; Cullen Skink from smoked haddock, milk, potatoes and onions; and creamy Partan Bree, made with crab. You may even come across Lorraine Soup on a menu. Prepared with chicken stock, lemon and nutmeg, it was popularized by Mary of Lorraine, mother of Mary Queen of Scots.

Main-course specialities include beef (steak on a menu will often specify Aberdeen Angus), lamb or mutton, game, such as

venison (low in cholesterol and very tasty), grouse and pheasant. Fresh fish and seafood should also feature on most good menus. In the towns along the coast, prawns, oysters, crabs and scallops are usually available, while inland, salmon is plentiful. Wild salmon is more expensive than the farmed type, but it has a much more delicate flavour. Trout is farmed in Scotland too, and often served fried in oatmeal and eaten with bacon. The firm pink flesh of the wild brown trout is as tasty as salmon.

Smoked haddock is a Scottish speciality – Arbroath Smokies and Finnan Haddies are the best-known varieties. The former are lightly salted, smoked over oak or birch wood and eaten warm. Finnan Haddies, from Findon in Aberdeenshire, are rubbed with salt, dried on the beach and then smoked over a peat fire. Kippers are herring which have been halved, salted and smoked. The best kippers are said to come from Loch Fyne.

Although haggis is described as the Scottish national dish, it is certainly not eaten every day and

Once distilled, whisky is left to mature in oak barrels for many years before it is bottled

The range of whiskies on offer is overwhelming

Scottish desserts are often smothered in butterscotch sauce or syrup. Cranachan, if properly made, is a delicious mixture of toasted oatmeal, whipped cream, whisky and raspberries. Atholl Brose is a variant of Cranachan. For a really filling dessert, try a Clootie Dumpling, a sweet and stodgy fruit pudding. Scotland is known for its soft fruits, especially the raspberries grown around Tayside which are said to be among the best in Europe.

A Scottish breakfast is as copious as the traditional English cooked breakfast, if not more so. Alongside your eggs and bacon, you may be given the additional choice of porridge, smokies or kippers, and oatcakes. Most of the larger hotels also offer a continental breakfast.

Tea-time is another important part of the day (especially on rainy days). This is your chance to taste authentic shortbread and Dundee cake and to sample a whole variety of other local tea-time treats.

Whisky may be the main export and it is drunk widely in Scotland, but the staple drink, after tea and coffee, is beer. A popular combination in Glasgow bars is a 'pint of heavy and a chaser', or a pint of ale and a whisky – only recommended for those with a strong constitution. A connoisseur of Scottish beer would claim

is not that easy to find in supermarkets, except towards the end of January when it is very much a part of the Burns' Night celebrations (see page 27). Made from the heart, liver and lungs of a sheep, mixed with suet, oatmeal and onion, then seasoned and sewn into a sheep's stomach, it is usually eaten with 'bashed neeps', mashed turnip, and washed down with whisky. Although it may not sound that appealing, it is definitely worth tasting.

The queen of Handa

In the last century 12 families lived on the island of Handa, which is now a bird reserve. It was ruled by its own 'queen', the oldest widow on the island. Handa had its own parliament, which assembled every morning in order to discuss and allocate the day's duties, most of which revolved around fishing, the collection of birds' eggs and the cultivation of potatoes.

that the brews produced north of the border are quite different to English beers. They generally have a sweeter taste and more body, but like English beers, they are served at room temperature. Scottish beers are graded by the shilling, a system used since the 1870s, which indicates the strength. The higher the shilling mark, the stronger or 'heavier' the beer. The biggest name brands are McEwan's, Youngers and Tennents, but there are many small local breweries that produce very fine strong ales. Traquair House in the Borders, for example, produces the wonderfully smooth House Ale, which is highly prized by beer connoisseurs. Continental beers and lagers are of course widely available in Scottish pubs, as is wine and all other spirits.

Every year, the Scottish Tourist Board publishes a booklet entitled *Taste of Scotland* which gives up-to-date information on hotels and restaurants that specialize in Scottish cooking. All types of international cuisine can also be found in the larger towns and cities. In the smaller towns and in the country restaurants and pubs, the choice on offer is much more limited. If you are out exploring during the day and want a quick snack, most pubs offer hot meals and sandwiches.

Edinburgh's pubs exude warmth and atmosphere

Harris tweeds and Islay malts

Wools and whiskies are the most popular buys

You will pass many more craft shops on a tour around Scotland than you will castles. In a country with over 50 million sheep, it is not surprising that hand-knitted jumpers and woollens invariably occupy prominent positions on the shelves of the souvenir shops. There are countless patterns and designs. Pringle is a classic label for jumpers, skirts, jackets and hats, but the best-known Scottish wool brand is, of course, Harris Tweed. The name was registered as a trademark as long ago as 1909. Any garment bearing the Harris Tweed label must comply with some very strict conditions: it must be made from pure Scottish wool (not necessarily from the island of Harris) and woven in the crofter's home on a hand loom. The original Harris tweeds were dyed with natural colours made from mosses and earth, but nowadays synthetic dyes are used. Authentic Harris Tweed jackets are expensive, but they are produced by highly skilled and hardworking craftspeople trying to make their living in the traditional way.

Many of the textile mills sell plaids in different tartan patterns. If you are interested in buying a tartan souvenir, it doesn't have to be a kilt; it could be a tie, a hat, a scarf or a pair of trousers – go directly to a woollen mill if you can. Souvenir shops and retailers in the town centres generally charge more.

Glass and pottery items make good souvenirs too. Edinburgh Crystal in Penicuik and Caithness Glass in Perth, Oban and Wick organize tours of their factories. Their shops display the glassware they produce, and they sell their goods at reasonable prices.

Other popular buys include jewellery made from local stone and objects carved from horn.

The choice of whisky on offer is quite overwhelming. As a general rule, single malts from the islands (Islay and Jura) are smoky, while Speyside malts tend to be much lighter and smoother. Glenmorangie and Glenfiddich are a safe bet for those who don't have an established preference.

Established in 1838, Jenners on Princes Street in Edinburgh is Scotland's answer to Harrods

Games and gatherings

Scotland's calendar is full of cultural festivals and sporting events

The ★ Highland Gatherings – the most famous of which is Braemar – are held in summer all over the country. Lively folk festivals and *ceilidhs* (pronounced 'kaylee') are held throughout the year. The Edinburgh Festival and the Glasgow Mayfest are the two main annual cultural events, which bring together performers and audiences from all around the world. Sheep-dog trials and horse shows, curling competitions and golfing championships all attract large crowds, while football and rugby are national obsessions.

PUBLIC HOLIDAYS

New Year's Day, Good Friday, May Day (1st Monday in May), *Christmas Day* and *Boxing Day* are all public holidays. Easter and Whitsun are religious festivals but, apart from Good Friday, are not celebrated as public holidays. Annual bank holidays are the same as in England, except for *St Andrew's Day* (30 Nov).

Bagpipe players at a military parade

FESTIVALS & LOCAL EVENTS

January
Burns' Night (25 Jan). Celebration of the national poet's birthday with Burns suppers all over Scotland – haggis, whisky and poetry.
Lerwick/Shetland: *Up Helly-Aa* (last Tuesday). Ancient Norse fire festival with torchlit procession culminating in the burning of a replica of a Viking longship.
Glasgow: *Celtic Connections* (late Jan or early Feb). International Gaelic music festival.

February
Scottish Curling Championships. At a different venue each year.
Inverness: *Music Festival* (last week).

March
Aviemore: *Cairngorm Snow Festival* (3rd weekend). Variety of events and competitions for adults and children, including skiing and snowboarding.

April
Lerwick/Shetland: *Folk Festival* (1st weekend).
Edinburgh: *Folk Festival* (early April). 10 days of music and dance.

MARCO POLO SELECTION: EVENTS

1 Edinburgh Festival
One of the world's leading cultural festivals for drama, dance, music, comedy and film. Book early for tickets and accommodation (page 29)

2 Highland Gatherings
A lively, colourful summer event held in various places throughout the country. Music and dancing, caber tossing and hammer-throwing (page 27)

Ayr: *Scottish Grand National* (mid-April).

Kirkcaldy: *Links Market* (3rd week). 6-day folk festival and funfair.

Tobermory/Isle of Mull: *Mull Music Festival* (last weekend). Concerts in the little island capital.

Rothesay/Isle of Bute: *Jazz Festival* (end of April, beginning of May). Well-known jazz musicians have been playing for years at this festival, located in the beautiful bathing town of Rothesay.

May

Stromness/Orkney: *Traditional Folk Festival* (3rd weekend). Musical events and *ceilidhs*.

Blair Castle, Perthshire: *Atholl Highlander's Parade* (late May). Annual parade of Scotland's only private army.

Glasgow: *International Jazz Festival* (end of May, beginning of June). The biggest jazz festival in all of Great Britain presents ten days of jazz music.

June

Isle of Arran: *Folk Festival* (2nd week). Traditional island festival.

Lochmaddy/North Uist: *Boat Festival* (3rd weekend). Sailing regattas, canoeing, white-water rafting; barbecues and children's events.

Kirkwall, Stromness/Orkney: *St Magnus Festival* (3rd week). 6-day arts festival: theatre, dance, readings, music and films.

Ingliston, near Edinburgh: *Royal Highland Show* (last week). Big agricultural show with many activities for children.

Dingwall: *Highland Traditional Music Festival* (late June).

Glasgow: *International Jazz Festival*, (late June to early July). One of Britain's best jazz events.

July

Isle of Tyree/Argyle: *Feis Thiriosh/Tyree Festival* (2nd week). Music and dancing, mostly Gaelic.

Isle of Barra: *Feis Bharraigh/Barra Festival* (2nd week). Gaelic music, dancing and plays.

Isle of Skye and Lochalsh: *Feis an Eilean/Skye and Lochalsh Festival* (2nd week). Variety of traditional Gaelic events.

Western Isles/Stornoway: *Hebridean Celtic Music Festival* (mid-July). Nationally and internationally known Celtic artists gather here in the Outer Hebrides for an annual celebration of their music heritage.

Eyemouth: *Herring Queen Festival* (late July to early Aug). Seafood festival with fishing boat procession, election of the herring queen and costume parade.

August

Parton (near Castle Douglas): *Alternative Games* (1st Sunday). Features 'tossin' the sheaf' and 'spinnin' the peerie'.

Fort William: *Glen Nevis River Race* (1st Sunday).

Edinburgh: *Military Tattoo*. Impressive spectacle of pipe bands and drums on the Castle Esplanade. Advance booking *Tel. 0131 225 1188, Fax 225 8627.*

Aberdeen: *International Youth Festival* (early Aug). 10-day festival for young, up-and-coming artists: classical music, jazz, theatre, singing and dancing.

St Andrews: *Lammas Fair* (early Aug). 5-day traditional fair.

Edinburgh: ★ *Edinburgh International Festival; Fringe Festival; International Film Festival.* Every August, all of Edinburgh is marked by the legendary theatre, dance, music, and comedy festival, which overlaps with the Fringe Festival and the International Film Festival. Early booking is highly recommended, both for hotels and tickets to performances.

– All of August: *The Fringe Festival,* once a leading forum for experimental work in the performing arts, has today become a highly regarded gathering featuring the best unaffiliated comedy, cabaret and theatre groups from all across Europe. Exhibitions and children's programmes are on offering here. Information: *Tel. 0131 226 52 57; Fax 220 42 05.*

– Mid-August, beginning of September: *The International Festival* is one of the most prominent theatre gatherings in all of Europe. Every year, the leading proponents of theatre and dance-theatre show their work in Scotland's capital city. Information: *Tel. 0131 226 40 01; Fax 225 11 73.* For tickets, call *0131 225 57 56.*

– Mid-August to late August: *The International Film Festival* shows new international work in film. Information: *Tel: 0131 228 40 51.*

Glasgow: *World Pipe Band Championships* (mid-August). The world's best bagpipe ensembles compete in Glasgow for international distinction.

Largs: *Largs Viking Festival* (end of August, beginning of September). This annual Viking festival features music, crafts, fireworks, and a mock Viking battle.

September

Braemar: *Royal Highland Gathering* (1st Saturday). Games in the presence of the royal family.

Tarbert: *Music Festival* (late Sept). Open air concerts and live music in hotels and on fishing boats.

Fort William: *Ben Nevis Race* to the top of Scotland's highest peak.

October

Aberdeen: *Alternative Festival.* 10-day festival of music, dancing, drama, workshops and comedy.

November

Dunvegan Castle/Isle of Skye: *Castle Fireworks* (1st Saturday). Spectacular display on the shores of Loch Dunvegan.

December

Kirkwall/Orkney: *Men's and Boys' Ba' Games.* Football for all on Christmas Day.

Edinburgh: *Hogmanay.* Huge New Year's Eve party all over the city.

The Borders and the Lowlands

Birthplace of Sir Walter Scott and Robert Burns

Throughout history, the border between Scotland and England has been an area of conflict and contention. Between the 13th and 17th centuries the surrounding territory, known as the Borders, was a regular battleground for two nations constantly at war. The countryside is scattered with the ruins of abbeys and fortresses – reminders of centuries of bitter fighting. The first real border, now in England, was demarcated by Hadrian's Wall. Built in AD 120-123 on the orders of the Roman Emperor Hadrian as a defence against the Picts and

The Ross Fountain, West Princes Street Gardens, in front of Edinburgh Castle

Scots, it was the northern frontier of Roman Britain for 250 years. It comprised a stone embankment with a ditch running below and extended for about 120 km (75 mi) from the Solway Firth in the west to the mouth of the river Tyne in the east. Parts of the wall are still standing, and you can walk along the top of it in places.

Southern Scotland can be subdivided into two areas: the Southern Uplands, encompassing the Cheviot Hills and Borders, and the Central Lowlands, stretching from the Firth of Clyde in the west to the Firth of Forth and Perth in the east.

Surprisingly, the Borders is the least visited region of Scotland, mainly because most tourists pass through it en route to the more

---

Hotel and restaurant prices

Hotels
Category 1: from £80
Category 2: from £50
Category 3: from £20
B&B: from £13
Prices per person in a double room with breakfast.

Restaurants
Category 1: from £35
Category 2: from £15
Category 3: from £8
Prices for a three-course meal. Drinks not included (wine is expensive).

popular Highlands and islands. The southern landscape may not be as dramatic, but it is varied and full of hidden treasures worth seeking out. Beyond the Cheviot Hills of the central Borders lie the attractive market towns of Jedburgh, Melrose, Kelso and Dryburgh, all of which boast splendid abbey ruins.

A little further north, but within easy reach of the Borders, lie Scotland's two main cities – Edinburgh on the eastern Lowland coast and Glasgow to the west. Edinburgh, the country's financial, legal and cultural centre, is one of the finest cities in Europe. Glasgow, Scotland's chief commercial and industrial centre, is a bit rougher around the edges, but a fascinating city nonetheless. Once a prosperous shipbuilding and engineering city, its days as a centre for heavy industry are now over, though there are still some shipyards and building rigs on Clydeside. It has undergone a massive regeneration programme over the last few years and, while it still has many social problems, its profile both nationally and internationally has vastly improved.

If you explore Dumfries, Galloway and the area around Ayr, you will come across the full range of landscapes typical of Scotland: remote mountain lakes, such as Loch Trool in Galloway Forest Park; vast expanses of wild moorland; and the gentle peaks of the Tweedsmuir and Pentland Hills. The scenery is as stunning here as it is anywhere in the northern part of Scotland. There are as many interesting castles and stately homes as in the Highlands, and some of the best places for walking, riding and fishing are in the south.

The *Robert Burns Heritage Trail* is a signposted route taking in the haunts of the Scottish bard. It is very popular, not only for its literary interest, but also for its scenic beauty. The trail starts in Alloway, the village where Burns was born. His family lived in a tiny, windowless cottage that they shared with their animals. Just beyond Alloway

The green rolling hills of southern Scotland

is the town of Ayr and the famous Tam o' Shanter Inn. Further south is Dumfries, where Burns spent the last years of his life.

It's worth bearing in mind when planning your holiday that during the peak period of July and August, the south-west is never as crowded as the central and western Highlands.

DUMFRIES

(104/B 6) This pleasant town (pop. 33,000) is on the tourist map mainly because of its connections with Robert Burns, who spent the last years of his life here. It also makes an excellent base for excursions into Galloway and along the shores of Solway Firth. The red sandstone houses give the town a warm and friendly atmosphere. Dumfries straddles the lovely River Nith, its two halves linked by the six-arched Devorguilla Bridge that dates from 1431.

A statue of Burns stands at the junction of High Street and Buccleuch Street.

SIGHTS

Burns Centre
Dating from 1781, this pretty mill on the River Nith houses an exhibition documenting the life of Scotland's national poet. There is also a bookshop and a café.
Mon-Sat 10.00-20.00, Sun 14.00-17.00; Mill Road

Burns' House
In 1791, Burns moved to Dumfries where he took a job as a tax collector. He had 15 children in all, six of whom were illegitimate, and he always struggled financially. He moved into the house in what was then called Mill Vennel in 1793, three years before he died, and his wife, Jean Armour, lived on here until 1834. Exhibits include manuscripts and letters.

MARCO POLO SELECTION: THE SOUTH

1 Abbotsford House
Home of Sir Walter Scott, Scotland's most celebrated writer (page 39)

2 Alloway
The birthplace of the Scottish bard Robert Burns (page 44)

3 Arran
Idyllic island often described as 'Scotland in miniature' (page 45)

4 Edinburgh
One of the finest and most elegant cities in Europe (page 35)

5 Glasgow
Once a great industrial centre, now a major cultural centre (page 41)

6 Glenkiln Reservoir
Works of art in a remote, natural setting (page 35)

7 Kelso
Delightful little town with an ancient abbey (page 40)

8 Loch Lomond
Britain's largest and perhaps most beautiful lake (page 45)

9 Melrose Abbey
Atmospheric abbey ruins (page 40)

On one of the bedroom windows you can see his signature, which he scratched into the wood with a diamond ring. The box-bed was the bed on which he died in 1796, aged just 37.

Mon-Sat 10.00-13.00 and 14.00-17.00, Sun 14.00-17.00; Burns Street

Burns' Mausoleum

Burns was buried in the grounds of St Michael's Church, not far from his home. In 1815 his body was moved into the mausoleum.

Globe Inn

❀ Burns' favourite *howff*, or pub, is still in business. Mementoes in this smoky, oak-panelled tavern include his favourite chair and a pane of glass with an engraving showing his portrait.

56 High Street

MUSEUMS

Dumfries Museum

Local history museum in a converted windmill. The main attraction is the camera obscura on the top floor, one of three in Scotland.

Mon-Sat 10.00-13.00 and 14.00-17.00, Sun 14.00-17.00

Old Bridge House Museum

A display of antique furniture and everyday objects. The building itself dates from 1660.

April-Sept Mon-Sat 10.00-13.00 and 14.00-17.00, Sun 14.00-17.00; Mill Road

RESTAURANT

Bruno's

Authentic and reasonably priced Italian food.

3 Balmoral Road; Category 3; Tel. 01387 55757

HOTELS

Comlongon Castle

Converted castle near Dumfries. Four-poster beds and gourmet cuisine. 12 rooms.

Category 1/2; Tel. 01387 870 283, Fax 870 266

Station Hotel

Friendly and comfortable hotel in an old Victorian building near the station. 32 rooms.

49 Lovers Walk; Category 2; Tel. 01387 244 316, Fax 250 388

INFORMATION

Dumfries Tourist Office

Whitesands; Tel. 01387 253 862

SURROUNDING AREA

Bruce's Stone   (103/E 5)

Loch Trool in Galloway Forest Park is the splendid setting for this memorial stone commemorating the victory of the Scottish hero, Robert the Bruce, over the English in 1307. Locally sold guidebooks give you details of the many walks, picnic areas and vantage points in the vicinity.

Caerlaverock Castle   (104/B 6)

The site of this beautiful moated castle was the seat of the Maxwell family. Built in around 1270, it underwent a number of alterations in the following centuries, most notably the addition of the Renaissance façade (1634).

April-Sept Mon-Sat 09.30-18.30, Sun 14.00-18.30

Ellisland Farm   (104/A-B 5)

Robert Burns leased this piece of farmland in 1788, but his crops failed and the land was auctioned

off in 1791. It was here that he wrote *Tam o' Shanter*, considered by many to be his greatest work. Items of Burns' memorabilia are displayed in the farmhouse. There are some nice walks from the museum along the Nith valley.
10 km (6 mi) north-west of Dumfries, off the A76

Glenkiln Reservoir   (104/A 5)

★ In an isolated spot north-west of Dumfries stand a number of impressive sculptures. Among them are Henry Moore's *King and Queen*, as well as works by Rodin, Epstein and others.
On the A75 towards Castle Douglas, turn-off after Shawhead

Gretna Green   (104/C 6)

This little village, just 16 km (10 mi) from the English border, was a refuge for desperate lovers until 1940, when marriage by declaration was made illegal. In the past, couples whose parents did not consent to their marriage would elope to Gretna Green where they could be married by declaration before a witness. The wedding vows were 'forged' over an anvil by the village blacksmith, whose shop now houses a museum and Visitor Centre.

Sweetheart Abbey   (104/B 6)

A beautiful monastic ruin south of Dumfries. The abbey was built in 1273 by Devorguilla Balliol in memory of her husband, John. In the nearby town of *New Abbey*, the *Shambellie House Museum of Costume* (*daily 11.00-17.00*) has a fine collection of clothes dating from Victorian times right up to the middle of this century.
April-Sept Mon-Sat 09.30-18.30, Sun 14.00-18.30

Threave Castle   (104/A 6)

This ruined 14th-century castle with its lovely gardens stands on a small island in the River Dee, not far from *Castle Douglas*. To reach the castle, you need to call the ferryman by ringing the bell at the river's edge.
Daily 09.30 until sunset

EDINBURGH

(105/D 2) ★ Scotland's capital (pop. 450,000) is one of the finest cities in Europe. All the main Scottish Office administration is carried out from here and it will become the seat of the new Scottish parliament in January 2000.

The natural focal point for visitors is ◁▷ Edinburgh Castle. It occupies a dominant position on a rocky outcrop to the south-west of the city centre and looks down on the historic Old Town.

The castle compound, with its massive walls and tightly-packed buildings, is almost a town in itself. To the east runs the Royal Mile, a medieval road leading to Holyrood Palace. This part of the city butts up to the New Town, now about 230 years old, on the north side of Princes Street. The architecture of this neighbourhood is impressive as a model of 18th-century planning. There are countless grand houses standing on imposing avenues and crescents, broad squares and attractive parks and gardens.

Work has begun on the construction of a parliament building. It was always thought in the past that the former Royal High School on Calton Hill, at the eastern end of Princes Street, would be converted to house the new assembly. But in January 1998, it was announced that a new parliament building would be erected next to Holyrood Palace. Robert the Bruce held a parliament on this very site in 1326.

Dean Village (O)
Once a milling centre, occupied by bakers, tanners and weavers, this area by the Water of Leith has been restored and many of the old mills converted into flats.
At the end of Queensferry Street

Edinburgh Castle (U/B 3–4)
All that remains of the earliest buildings erected on this rocky crag is *St Margaret's Chapel* (12th century). In the vaults beneath the *Great Hall* on *Crown Square* is the medieval *Mons Meg* cannon which used to stand on the battlements. On the eastern side of the square is the *Palace* where, in a tiny room, Mary Queen of Scots gave birth to James VI, who became James I of England. In a neighbouring room, the magnificent *Honours of Scotland* (Scottish Crown Jewels) are now displayed alongside the *Stone of Scone* (or Stone of Destiny), restored to the castle in 1996. The *Scottish National War Memorial* and the *Scottish United Services Museum* are part of the complex.
Daily 09.30-17.15

Outlook Tower and Camera Obscura (U/C 3–4)
The 17th-century tower at the end of the Esplanade houses a camera obscura, projecting images of Edinburgh from 1850. On a clear day, the telescopes and viewfinders on the roof offer some of the best views of the city.
Daily 09.30-18.00; Castle Hill

Palace of Holyroodhouse (O)
The north tower was built for James IV in the 16th century, but the rest of the building is 17th century. The ornate state rooms are open to the public and worth a visit. In the picture gallery hang 89 of the original 110 portraits of Scottish rulers (some of them fictitious) all by the Dutch master Jacob De Wet, who painted them in just two years. The most interesting part of the palace is Mary Queen of Scots' apartments in the north-west tower. It was here that her Italian secretary and alleged lover, Rizzio, was brutally stabbed to death. The palace is the official residence of the Queen when she visits Scotland (*Mon-Sat 09.30-17.15, Sun until 16.30*).

After visiting the palace, you can take a stroll up to *Arthur's Seat* (250 m/822 ft) in nearby Holyrood Park. The wind may be bracing, but the view is fantastic.

The royal arms

Royal Mile

The Royal Mile, actually made up of four consecutive streets, leads from Edinburgh Castle down to Holyrood Palace. As you walk down this long stretch lined with 17th-century grey stone houses, you will pass the following places of interest: *Lady Stairs House* (1622) (**U/C 3**), which contains manuscripts and memorabilia of Scott, Burns and Stevenson; *Lawnmarket* (**U/C–D 3**); *St Giles Cathedral* (15th century) (**U/D 3**); *High Street* (**U/D-E 3**); the *Museum of Childhood* (**U/E 3**); *John Knox's House* (**U/E3**); *Huntly House* (**U/F3**), a museum of local history; and the *People's Story* (**U/F3**), a museum showing the everyday life of the people of Edinburgh.

The house of the Scottish reformer, John Knox

MUSEUMS

Georgian House (U/A 2–3)

This fine museum is in a grand town house on Charlotte Square. It was designed by Robert Adam and built in 1791 and still contains the original furnishings.
Mon-Sat 10.00-17.00, Sun 14.00-17.00; 7 Charlotte Square

National Gallery of Scotland (U/C 3)

One of the best art galleries in Europe with works by Rubens, Rembrandt, Holbein, Titian, Raphael, French Impressionists and Scottish and English masters.
Mon-Sat 10.00-17.00, Sun 14.00-17.00; The Mound

Royal Museum of Scotland (U/D 4)

An interesting museum with a varied collection of archaeological, geological and ethnological exhibits covering all eras and aspects of Scottish life.
Mon-Sat 10.00-17.00, Sun 12.00-17.00; Chambers Street

Scottish National Gallery of Modern Art (O)

A fine modern art collection, including works by Henry Moore, David Hockney, Picasso and Mondrian, in a stylish 19th-century house set in lovely grounds.
Mon-Sat 10.00-17.00, Sun 14.00-17.00; Belford Road, on the outskirts

Scottish National Portrait Gallery (U/C–D 1)

Collection of portraits, mainly of famous Scots from the 16th century to the present day.
Mon-Sat 10.00-17.00, Sun 14.00-17.00; corner of Queen Street and Dublin Street

RESTAURANTS & PUBS

The Abbotsford (U/C 2)

Good, inexpensive and always busy. Original Victorian fittings.
3 Rose Street; Category 3; Tel. 0131 225 5276

The Black Bull (U/C 4)

✦ This pub below the castle serves excellent malt whisky and fine ale. Scottish musicians often play here.
12 Grassmarket; Category 3; Tel. 0131 225 6636

Dubh Prais (U/E 3)

Scottish food at its best in a cosy, intimate setting.
123b High Street; Category 2; Tel. 0131 557 5732

The Witchery (U/C 4)

Gourmet restaurant with a great atmosphere. Excellent wine list.
Castle Hill, Royal Mile; Category 1; Tel. 0131 225 5613

SHOPPING

Princes Street (**U/A–D 3–2**) is Scotland's premier shopping street with all the main retail outlets. *Jenners* is a long-established department store. Below ground, at the upper end near Waverley Station, is the *Waverley Shopping Centre* (**U/D 3**), which boasts about 60 shops and several restaurants. *Rose Street* (**U/A–C 3–2**), running parallel to Princes Street, is a pedestrian zone. If you are looking for something typically Scottish to take home or give as a present, such as clothing, food, drink or antiques, then the *Royal Mile* (**U/C–E 3**) and the roads around *Grassmarket* (**U/C 4**) have the biggest selection of shops.

HOTELS

Adria (O)

A friendly family hotel with sizeable rooms in peaceful surroundings. 23 rooms.
11-12 Royal Terrace; Category 2; Tel. 0131 556 7875, Fax 558 7782

Carlton Highland Hotel (U/D 3)

Large traditional hotel with luxurious rooms and several restaurants. 197 rooms.
North Bridge; Category 1; Tel. 0131 556 7277, Fax 556 2691

Osbourne Hotel (U/D 1)

Located in the centre of the city. Clean and friendly. 50 rooms.
59 York Place; Category 2; Tel. 0131 556 5577, Fax 556 1012

Pollock Halls of Residence (O)

Student accommodation open to the public during vacation periods – from March to April and June to September. 500 rooms.
18 Holyrood Park; Category 3; Tel. 0131 667 0662, Fax 662 9479

Queen Margaret College (O)

Cheap beds, normally used by students. Available from June to September. 428 rooms.
Clerwood Terrace; Category 3; Tel. 0131 317 3310, Fax 317 3256

Stuart House (O)

Pretty Georgian building near the city centre. Nicely furnished. Non-smokers only. 7 rooms.
12 East Claremont Street; Category 2; Tel. 0131 557 9030, Fax 557 0563

ENTERTAINMENT

Edinburgh is a major venue for international events, so you'll find plenty of possibilities when planning your evenings out.

Every day from April to October, traditional Scottish banquets are held in the *King James Hotel* the *Scandic Crown Hotel* and the *Carlton Highland Hotel*. Nightclubs and discos such as ✦ *Au Bar* (*101 Shandwick Place*) (**U/A 3**), *The Kitchen* (*245 Cowgate*) (**U/D–E 4**) or *The*

Tunnel (*16 Forrest Road*) (**U/D4**) are open until dawn. Theatre-lovers will be delighted. *The Kings Theatre, Leven Street* (**U/B6**), *The Playhouse Theatre, Grenside Place* (**U/E1**), *The Royal Lyceum, Grindlay Street* (**U/A4**) and *St Bride's Centre* have a reputation for good productions, though you may have difficulty getting a seat at short notice.

Up-to-date information and full entertainment listings are found in *What's on in Edinburgh*, available from the tourist office.

It is advisable to buy tickets for the theatre and festival events in advance. Further information and brochures can be obtained from the tourist office.

3 Princes Street, Waverly Market; Tel. 0131 557 1700, Fax 557 5118

SURROUNDING AREA

Abbotsford House   (105/D 4)

★ This section of the River Tweed flanked by rolling hills is known as Scott Country. It was here that the great novelist, Sir Walter Scott (1771-1832), lived. He renamed the palatial home he built 1817-25 Abbotsford House, for he was none too keen on the original name for the farmland he purchased in 1811, which was Cartley (meaning dirty) Hole. The study where he penned so many of his works, his library and the Knights' Hall all remain as he left them. Of particular interest is his collection of curios which includes a lock of Bonnie Prince Charlie's hair and a pair of Robert Burns' glasses.

End of March-Oct, Mon-Sat 10.00-17.00, Sun 14.00-17.00

Cheviot Hills   (105/E-F 5)

These gently rolling hills form Scotland's southern border. The flocks of sheep, quiet villages and narrow streets are the perfect introduction to the rural charm of Scotland. Excellent walking and horse riding country.

Culross   (104/B-C 1)

Most of this well-preserved little town by the Firth of Forth belongs to the National Trust. Many of the houses date from the 16th and 17th centuries. The *Town House, Study, Palace* (*Easter-Sept, daily 11.00-16.00*) and the *Abbey* are the principal sights. Details available from the Visitor Centre.

Dryburgh Abbey   (105/E 4)

This ruined abbey by the River Tweed was built by the Premonstratensian monks in 1150. Sir Walter Scott's tomb lies here.

Mon-Sat 09.30-18.30, Sun 14.00-18.30

Hopetoun House   (104/C 1)

Built between 1699 and 1703, this magnificent Baroque mansion was later extended by William Adam and completed by his son, Robert, in 1767. The house and grounds merge with the surrounding countryside to create an impressive whole. The landscaped gardens were based on those at Versailles.

Easter-Oct, daily 10.00-17.30

Jedburgh Abbey   (105/E 4)

The ruins of this monastery church were once part of the powerful Augustinian abbey built in 1138. The town itself is picturesque and has a visitor centre.

Mon-Sat 09.30-18.30, Sun 14.00-18.30

Kelso (105/E 4)

★ A charming town (pop. 5400) in a pretty spot at the confluence of the Tweed and Teviot rivers. The ruined shell of *Kelso Abbey* is all that remains of what was once the largest abbey in the Borders. It was founded in 1128 by Augustinian monks who had been invited to establish a monastery by King David I.

Linlithgow Palace (104/C 1)

Built in 1425, this well-preserved palace was the favourite residence of the Stewart kings and the birthplace of Mary Queen of Scots. It stands by a lake in a beautiful park in the little town of *Linlithgow*, west of Edinburgh.
Mon-Sat 09.30-18.30, Sun 14.00-18.30

Melrose Abbey (105/D 4)

★ The ruined arches, windows and towers of this 12th-century Cistercian monastery stand in the Tweed valley. Like most of the other abbeys in this area, it was repeatedly sacked by the English.
Mon-Sat 09.30-18.30, Sun 14.00-18.30

North Berwick (105/E 2)

Just off the North Sea resort of North Berwick (golf and water sports) lies *Bass Rock*. A landmark for sailors, this volcanic rock is home to thousands of birds, especially gannets, but also puffins, fulmars, kittiwakes and guillemots. Cruises out to the rock leave from North Berwick harbour (*for times and fares, enquire at the tourist office*). Nearby you can see the dramatic ruin of *Tantallon Castle* (14th century), seat of the powerful Douglas clan (*Mon-Sat 09.30-18.30, Sun 14.00-18.30*).

Rosslyn Chapel (105/D 2–3)

The 15th-century chapel in Roslin was built by the master mason, William St Clair. Originally in-

George Square and Glasgow's town hall

tended as a vast cruciform collegiate church, the building was never finished. It boasts some imaginative carvings, including the richly decorated Prentice Pillar. One of the finest places of worship in Scotland.

April-Oct Mon-Sat 10.00-17.00, Sun 12.00-16.45

Thirlestane Castle (105/D 3)

Splendid castle near *Lauder* on the A68. It houses the *Border Country Life Museum* which focuses on the region's history.

May, June and Sept open Mon, Tues, Thurs, Sun 14.00-17.00; July/Aug daily (except Sat) 14.00-17.00

Traquair House (104/C 3–105/D 3)

Parts of this huge mansion near *Innerleithen* date from the 10th century, making Traquair House the oldest building in Scotland to have been continuously inhabited. Many Scottish and English rulers have stayed here over the years. The strong ales brewed in the adjoining brewery are highly prized by beer enthusiasts.

April, May, June and Sept daily 12.30-17.30; July/Aug daily 10.30-17.30; Oct, Sat/Sun 12.30-17.30

GLASGOW

(103/F 1) ★ The largest city in Scotland (pop. 755,000), and Edinburgh's old rival, is currently undergoing a renaissance. It is no longer a major shipbuilding and heavy engineering centre, and has shed its image as a city of slums and crime. Thanks largely to an effective campaign run in the early 1980s under the slogan 'Glasgow's miles better', the city is now brimming with enterprise and vitality. Trade and commerce

shaped Glasgow in the past, and today the search for new economic outlets has led the city to forge closer links with Europe. Now a modern cultural capital, it has some of the best museums and galleries in Britain, not to mention some wonderful 19th-century architecture. Public and private money has been poured into urban renewal projects; many of the fine Victorian buildings have been renovated and new buildings erected.

The area around the city is worth exploring, especially *Pollok Country Park*. Drive or cruise along the River Clyde, and see where such famous ocean liners as the *Queen Elizabeth* were built. Loch Lomond is only a short drive away.

SIGHTS

Bellahouston Park

In August this fine park, much admired for its colourful flowers, is the venue for the international bagpipe championships. In its grounds is the *Art Lover's House*, built to a design by Charles Rennie Mackintosh.

City Chambers (Town Hall)

At the heart of the city is the busy *George Square* which is lined with imposing 19th-century buildings and dotted with statues, dominated by the Sir Walter Scott column. The most impressive of these grand Victorian buildings is *City Chambers*, erected in 1888 in the Italian Renaissance style. Among the most interesting features of its lavish interior are the loggia, the marble staircase and mosaic floor.

Mon-Fri 10.30–15.30

Glasgow Cathedral

The city's fine Gothic cathedral dates from the 12th century and is the only one in Scotland to have survived the Reformation intact. The first chapel on the site was founded in 543 by St Mungo, patron saint of Glasgow. His tomb is enshrined in the vaulted crypt (Lower Church), architecturally the most interesting part of the building. Given its position on the hill, it was necessary to build the cathedral on two levels. *Mon-Sat 09.30-13.00 and 14.00-18.00, Sun 14.00-17.00.*

Glasgow School of Art

One of Charles Rennie Mackintosh's (1868-1928) finest buildings, designed by the architect while he was still a student at the college. *Guided tours: Mon-Fri mornings; 167 Renfrew Street*

Mitchell Library

Founded in 1874 by the tobacco merchant Stephen Mitchell, the library houses over a million volumes and is the largest of its kind in western Europe. The collection includes early volumes of works by Burns. *Mon-Fri 09.30-21.00, Sat 09.30-17.00; North Street*

Necropolis

Packed together on a hill to the east of the Cathedral lie the remains of the city's great and good. ☙ The site offers a fine view of the city.

Provand's Lordship

This beautifully furnished house is the oldest in Glasgow (1471). *Mon-Sat 10.00-17.00, Sun 11.00-17.00; 3 Castle Street*

University of Glasgow

Glasgow University (next to Kelvingrove Park) was founded in 1451. As well as the faculty buildings, the campus also contains the *Hunterian Museum* and the *Hunterian Art Gallery*, with its reconstruction of Mackintosh's home (see: Museums). *Mon-Sat 09.30-17.00, Sun 14.00-17.00; University Avenue*

West End

The *Park Conservation Area* dates from the 19th century and is of great architectural interest. It includes the crescents on the hill above Kelvingrove Park, namely Park Circus, Woodlands Terrace and Terrace Park; the university in the West End; and to the north, the *Botanic Garden* (*daily 07.00-sunset*) with its celebrated orchid collection. *Kibble Palace* (*daily 10.00-16.45*) is a Victorian conservatory best known for its ferns.

Willow Tea Rooms

Everything from the decor and high-backed chairs to the menu and teaspoons was designed by Mackintosh. A delightful spot for afternoon tea. *Mon-Sat 09.30-16.30; 217 Sauchiehall Street*

MUSEUMS & GALLERIES

Art Lover's House

Built to a design draughted by Mackintosh, it took seven years to complete this art gallery which was finally opened in 1996, complete with Art Nouveau fittings. It is mainly used as a study centre for art students. *Sat/Sun 10.00-17.00, weekdays by appt.; Bellahouston Park; Tel. 0141 353 4770.*

Burrell Collection

A visit to the Burrel Collection is a must both for the works and the building (1983) itself. It is set in a delightful location in the middle of Pollok Country Park. The collection was donated to the city by wealthy industrialist, Sir William Burrell (1861-1958). By the time he died he had amassed a vast array of artworks from around the world. Among the highlights are the French paintings, glass, tapestries and Chinese ceramics.
Mon-Sat 10.00-17.00, Sun 11.00-17.00

Gallery of Modern Art

Recently opened art gallery housed in an 18th-century mansion. The works are arranged on four levels around the themes of earth, air, fire and water.
Mon-Sat 10.00-17.00, Sun 11.00-17.00; Queen Street

Hunterian Art Gallery

The small but fine collection includes works by Whistler and a number of Glasgow painters. The gallery also features a reconstruction of Mackintosh's home.
Mon-Sat 09.30-17.00; University Hillhead Street

Kelvingrove Art Gallery and Museum

This impressive red sandstone building in Kelvingrove Park dates from 1902. It houses one of Europe's finest art collections including works by Italian masters, 17th-century Flemish masters, paintings by Degas, Monet and Bonnard among other French greats, and a selection of fine works by Scottish artists.
Mon-Sat 10.00-17.00, Sun 11.00-17.00; Argyle Street, Kelvingrove

Museum of Transport

The collection ranges from horse-drawn carriages and steam engines to Jackie Stewart's racing car and models of the luxury ocean liners built in Glasgow's shipyards.
Mon-Sat 10.00-17.00, Sun 11.00-17.00; Kelvin Hall, Bunhouse Road

People's Palace

This museum is situated in *Glasgow Green* by the River Clyde, the city's first public park (1662). The exhibits provide a fascinating insight into the history of the city. Stop off for refreshments in the exotic *Winter Gardens*.
Mon-Sat 10.00-17.00, Sun 11.00-17.00

Pollok House

A fine example of a Scottish stately home brimming with art treasures. In Pollok Country Park.
Mon-Sat 10.00-17.00, Sun 11.00-17.00; Near the Burrell Collection

St Mungo Museum of Religious Life and Art

Unique collection focusing on the sacred art of world religions.
Mon-Sat 10.00-17.00, Sun 11.00-17.00; Near the Cathedral

RESTAURANTS

The Admiral

❦ Smart pub with a nautical feel right in the heart of the city.
72a Waterloo Street; Category 3; Tel. 0141 221 7705

Harry Ramsden's

❦ This chain of restaurants prides itself on the quality of its fish and chips. It claims to be the largest restaurant of its kind in the world.
251 Paisley Road; Category 3; Tel. 0141 429 3700

Rogano

Famous Art Nouveau fish restaurant (1876) whose interior is a replica of the *Queen Mary* luxury liner. First class cuisine.
11 Exchange Place; Category 1/2; Tel. 0141 248 4055

Ubiquitous Chip

Sample original Scottish dishes in the covered courtyard or inside. Good wine list.
12 Ashton Lane (West End); Category 2; Tel. 0141 334 5007

SHOPPING

Buchanan Street, a pedestrianized area in the centre of the city, is the main shopping street. The old sandstone building at *48 Princes Square* has been converted into a modern shopping centre and the vast, glass-roofed *St Enoch Square Shopping Centre* on *Argyll Street* is another bustling shopping mall. *Frasers* is Glasgow's best department store and the city also boasts one of the largest street markets in Scotland (*Sat and Sun 09.00-17.00; Barras Enterprise Trust, Unit 1, 54 Calton Entry*).

HOTELS

Aldara Guest House

Friendly, family-run guest house in a quiet spot near Kelvingrove Park. Basic level of accommodation. 6 rooms.
5 Bentick Street; Category 3; Tel. 0141 339 0852

Devonshire Hotel

Delightful interior. Every comfort, plus the best location in the West End. 16 rooms.
5 Devonshire Gardens; Category 1; Tel. 0141 339 7878, Fax 339 3980

Kirklee Hotel

Elegant Victorian premises in a quiet location near the university. 9 rooms.
11 Kensington Gate; Category 2; Tel. 0141 334 5555, Fax 339 3828

ENTERTAINMENT

✷ ❖ Voted 'European City of Culture' in 1990 and set to be the 'City of Architecture and Design' in 1999, Glasgow enjoys a reputation of world renown and has a lot to offer in the way of entertainment.

The theatres stage a wide range of productions. They include the *Citizens Theatre* (*Gorbals Street*), the splendid *Kings Theatre* (*Bath Street*), the *Theatre Royal* (*Hope Street*), the *Tron Theatre* (*Albert Drive*) and the *Royal Scottish Academy of Music and Drama* (*Renfrew Street*).

There are plenty of nightclubs, discos and jazz clubs. *King Tut's Wah Wah Hut* (*daily from 22.00; 272a St Vincent Street; Tel. 0141 221 5279*) is a popular rock music venue.

INFORMATION

Tourist Information Centre

11 George Square, Glasgow G1 2ER; Tel. 0141 204 4400, Fax 221 3524

SURROUNDING AREA

Alloway   (103/E 3)

★ Birthplace of the Scottish national poet, Alloway is a place of pilgrimage for Robert Burns enthusiasts. *Burns' Cottage and Museum* (*daily 09.00-20.00*) and the *Tam o'Shanter Experience* (*daily 10.00-20.00*) are the two main attractions. To explore other nearby Burns' haunts, follow the *Burns Heritage Trail*, which starts in Ayr,

*The birthplace of Robert Burns –
a place of pilgrimage for many Scots*

at the *Tam o' Shanter Inn* (*230 High Street*) where Burns used to drink, and continues right through Galloway to Dumfries.

Arran (102/C 1–2, 103/D 1–2)
★ To reach this pretty island with its varied landscape, take the ferry from the port of Ardrossan on the Firth of Clyde. If you are coming from the north, take the ferry from Claonaig on the Kintyre peninsula to Lochranza. Arran never gets too crowded and is ideal for hill-walkers. Accommodation is available in family-run bed and breakfasts and small hotels. *Brodick Castle* is worth a visit for the pretty grounds (*Easter-Sept daily 11.30-17.00, Oct Sat/Sun 13.00-17.00*).

Chatelherault Country Park (103/F 2)
The Duke of Hamilton's hunting lodge was built in 1732 by William Adam. It lies in a lovely park and has been superbly restored (*daily 10.30-16.30*).

Cloch Lighthouse (115/E 5)
◁▷ The view from this lighthouse south-west of Gourock covers the whole of the Clyde estuary.

Culzean Castle and Country Park (103/D 3)
This grand 18th-century castle was built by Robert Adam in the Classical style he favoured. The outbuildings and much of the interior are also Adam's work. Features of interest in the splendid park include an orangery, ponds and an aviary.
Castle: April-Oct, daily 10.30-17.30; Grounds: 09.30 to sunset

Helensburgh (107/E 5)
The highlight of this little town on the right bank of the Clyde is *Hill House* (1902-03), built by Charles Rennie Mackintosh.
Daily 13.30-17.30; Upper Colquhoun Street

Kirkoswald (103/D 5)
This village straddles the A77 to Stranraer and is best known for *Souter Johnnie's Cottage* – the home of the village cobbler who was Tam's drinking partner in *Tam o' Shanter*. Life-sized statues of the souter, Tam, the innkeeper and his wife can be seen in the restored alehouse in the garden.
Daily 13.30-17.30; beyond Maybole

Loch Lomond (107/E–F 4–5)
★ Loch Lomond, 40 km (25 mi) long and 8 km (5 mi) wide, is the largest lake in Great Britain. A leisurely cruise on a pleasure boat around the lake affords some fine views of the surroundings. Nearby is the peak of ◁▷ *Ben Lomond* (947 m/3125 ft high). It's a 4-hour walk from Rowardennan to the top of the ben and back again.

The heart of Scotland

*From Stirling Castle to Loch Ness, the beauty
of the Highlands gradually unfolds*

Just an hour's drive from either Edinburgh or Glasgow, the Highlands begin. Stirling, with its imposing castle, is generally considered to be the main gateway to the region. In earlier times, Stirling Bridge was the most important River Forth crossing, giving access to the Grampian Mountains. Beyond Stirling and Perth, the A9 via Glen Garry leads to the west of the Central Highlands, while the A93 via Glen Shee leads north. Striking views accompany you along the way: an endless horizon of rusty brown hills and moorland, blanketed in a sea of purple heather in mid-summer, and shimmering lochs that are steel blue in the sun and black as night when the sky is overcast.

At 670 m (2211 ft), Cairnwell Pass (A93) is the highest road pass in Britain. Beyond it, past the snaking bends of Devil's Elbow is Glen Clunie. Suddenly, the inhospitable terrain turns into a rural idyll, where the River Dee flows eastward through the val-

The ruins of fairy-tale castles are a common sight in the glens

ley. This area is known as Royal Deeside, being close to Braemar where Balmoral, the royal family's holiday home, is located. Ballater and Banchory are other holiday resorts in the valley, which extends as far as Aberdeen, Scotland's third largest city. Originally, it stood at the mouth of the river (*aber* means 'mouth') but it has gradually expanded, spreading both inland and to the north of the river. Aberdeen is certainly worth a visit, but it is the castles in the area around it – such as Castle Fraser, Crathes Castle and Craigievar Castle – that make this such a fascinating region.

The other route via Glen Garry (A9) passes Pitlochry and Blair Castle and on to Strathspey, the valley of the River Spey. Just beyond the Cairngorm Mountains lies Aviemore, Britain's leading winter sports resort. If you are searching for seclusion and tranquillity, this busy tourist area is not for you. The Highland Folk Museum in Kingussie and the Highland Wildlife Park near Kincraig are less hectic, and there is no shortage of opportunities for hill walking around here.

Another attraction in this part of the Grampian region are the whisky distilleries. Many of the famous centres of whisky production are found around Dufftown, known as the 'Malt Whisky Capital of the World'. All the distilleries offer guided tours (usually free).

In the north-west of the Central Highlands is Inverness, 'Capital of the Highlands', the battlefield of Culloden and Loch Ness.

ABERDEEN

(**115/E 6**) Much of Aberdeen (pop. 187,000) is built of local granite and its buildings are predominantly grey. However, this North Sea city is not as dull as many claim. It is a lively and prosperous centre with a very low rate of unemployment. Local industries include shipbuilding, heavy engineering, the chemical industry and, of course, North Sea oil. Fishing also remains a viable source of employment. Aberdeen has kept its reputation as a solid, upright city whose inhabitants are open and friendly. Although the east coast has none of the rugged splendour of the west coast and most of the tourist attractions lie inland, it is worth travelling the extra miles to see 'The Silver City'.

SIGHTS

Duthie Park, Winter Gardens
This park has the largest glasshouse in Europe: a steamy jungle paradise with enormous cacti, all sorts of exotic plant and tropical bird. It also features a wonderful Japanese water garden. A good place for a rainy day.
Daily 10.00 until sunset; Polmuir Road/Riverside Drive

Fish Market
✪ Every day hundreds of tonnes of fish are brought into the city

Aberdeen is one of the biggest fishing ports in Britain

MARCO POLO SELECTION: THE CENTRAL HIGHLANDS

1 Achray Forest Drive
Follow the forest tracks deep into the heart of the Highlands (page 58)

2 Blair Castle
The seat of the Duke of Atholl houses a splendid collection of historic exhibits (page 59)

3 Culloden Moor
The Battle of Culloden marked the beginning of the end for the clans (page 55)

4 Glamis Castle
Closely linked with the royal family (page 60)

5 Glen Affric
An isolated, but beautiful valley (page 54)

6 Highland Wildlife Park
The wild animals that once roamed free throughout the Highlands can now be seen in the 100-hectare grounds of the park (page 55)

7 Leith Hall
A beautiful mansion with fine gardens (page 51)

8 Queen Elizabeth Forest Park
A magnificent, unspoilt expanse of Highland Scotland (page 61)

9 Stirling Castle
This castle stands on a dominant rocky crag and has been a focal point of Scottish history through the ages (page 57)

and auctioned at one of Britain's largest fishing ports.
Best time: Mon-Fri 07.00-08.00; near Market Street

Mercat Cross
Large market cross (1686) carved with portraits of the Stewart kings.
Castlegate

Old Aberdeen
North of the modern city centre lies the old heart of the city, a separate entity until 1891 with its own council and charter. It is best explored on foot. Places of interest include *St Machar's Cathedral* (14th century), *St Andrew's Cathedral* (1784), *King's College Chapel* (1495) and *Brig o' Balgownie*, a 14th-century bridge that spans the River Don.

MUSEUMS

Aberdeen Art Gallery
A lively arts centre with a good collection of British paintings covering three centuries. Exhibitions and cultural events are held here.
Mon-Sat 10.00-17.00, Thurs 10.00-20.00, Sun 14.00-17.00; Schoolhill

Marischal Museum
A fine anthropological museum in Marischal College, near the 80 m (264 ft) high Mitchell Tower.
Daily (except Sat) 10.00-17.00; Broad Street

Maritime Museum
Maritime history and the story of North Sea oil are told in one of Aberdeen's oldest houses (1593).
Mon-Sat 10.00-17.00; Shiprow

Provost Skene's House

This 16th-century house was the residence of the Provost of Aberdeen. Furnished in period style, it features a fine gallery and a museum of local history.
Mon-Sat 10.00-17.00; Broad Street

RESTAURANTS

Ashvale

Delicious fresh fish dishes.
46 Great Western Road; Category 2/3; Tel. 01224 596 981

Silver Darling

Scottish produce prepared with a little French flair.
North Pier, Pocra Quay; Category 2; Tel. 01224 576 229

SHOPPING

Union Street is the main shopping street. *Grandholm Mills* at Woodside, Scotland's largest wool mill, has a good shop; it is located about 5 km (3 mi) from the city centre heading north-west (A96).

HOTELS

Atholl Hotel

Comfortable family hotel in a Victorian building. 35 rooms.
54 Kings Gate; Category 2; Tel. 01224 323 505, Fax 321 555

Caledonian Thistle Hotel

Stylishly decorated hotel in the city centre. 80 rooms.
Union Terrace; Category 2; Tel. 01224 640 233, Fax 641 627

Strathboyne Guest House

Pretty house, not far from the city centre. 7 rooms.
26 Abergeldie Terrace; Category 3; Tel. 01224 593 400

INFORMATION

Tourist Information Centre

St Nicholas House, Broad Street; Tel. 01224 632 727, Fax 644 822

SURROUNDING AREA

Balmoral Castle   (114/B 6)

In 1848 Queen Victoria fell in love with the Scottish Highlands, so in 1852 her husband, Prince Albert, bought Balmoral Castle and commissioned the architect William Smith to rebuild it in Baronial style. The royal family first used it in 1855 and it has been used as a royal retreat ever since.
Gardens and art exhibition, May-July Mon-Sat 10.00-17.00; closed Sun and while the royal family are in residence

Banff   (115/D 3)

Of special interest in this old, well-restored coastal town is the elegant *Duff House* designed by William Adam.
Daily 10.00-17.00

Braemar   (114/B 6)

Village in the Dee valley, best known for the ✪ Royal Highland Games held in September. Romantic *Braemar Castle* was rebuilt after a fire in 1748.
Easter-Oct daily (except Fri) 10.00-18.00

Castle Fraser   (115/D 5-6)

This grand and imposing castle standing at the end of an avenue was built between 1575 and 1636. It is a fine example of the tower-house style and features unusual decorative details. The *Great Hall* is particularly impressive.
July/Aug 11.00-17.30, otherwise 13.30-18.00

Balmoral Castle: the royal retreat

Craigievar Castle (114/C 6)

Hugely popular fairy-tale castle built by a local entrepreneur in 1626, in extravagant Baronial style. Access is limited.

Crathes Castle (115/D 6)

Built between 1533 and 1660, this castle, with its beautifully painted oak ceilings (1599) and period furniture, is another fine example of the tower-house style. The splendid gardens were designed in the 20th century by Lady Burnett.
April-Oct daily 11.00-17.30; Gardens: 09.30 until sunset

Dunnottar Castle (109/F 2)

Impressive 14th-century ruined fortress by the sea, near *Stonehaven*. The Scottish Regalia were kept here until the castle was besieged by Cromwell, but Scottish patriots smuggled the crown, sceptre and sword out to safety.
Mon-Sat 09.00-18.00, Sun 14.00-18.00

Fraserburgh (115/F 4–114/C 3)

Busy port with Scotland's oldest lighthouse. Long sandy beach and a delightful coast to the west.

Huntly Castle (115/D 4)

This imposing ruin was the seat of the powerful Gordon clan until the 17th century. Destroyed on several occasions, it was last rebuilt in 1602.
Mon-Sat 09.30-18.30, Sun 14.00-18.30

Leith Hall (114/C 5)

★ An enchanting castle set in extensive grounds where cattle and sheep graze. The gardens' attractive features include a zigzag herbaceous border, a rock garden, a pond walk and a picnic area.
Easter-Sept daily 13.30-17.30; Garden: 09.30 until sunset all year round

Tomintoul (114/B 5)

〽️ The second highest village in the Highlands lies along a ridge flanked on one side by the River Avon, famous for its crystal-clear water, and on the other by Conglass Water. The surrounding area is perfect walking country, and the *Lecht Tow* ski centre is nearby.

INVERNESS

(113/E 3) Inverness (pop. 60,000) lies between the Central and Northern Highlands, with the Moray Firth on the east side and Loch Ness to the west. The 'Capital of the Highlands' is a major tourist centre. Crowned by a pink sandstone castle, Inverness has kept much of its original medieval layout. From the top of Castle Hill, there is a beautiful view of the Highland slopes.

Attractive rows of houses run along the river, on the east side of which towers the cathedral. It is in this part of the town that you will find most bed and breakfasts. About a mile or so upriver is Ness Islands, an attractive public park that can be reached via the Edwardian bridges. The fast-flowing River Ness is rich with salmon and popular with anglers.

Upstream, the Ness runs parallel to the Caledonian Canal. Designed in the 19th century by Thomas Telford, this extensive waterway links Inverness, Loch Ness, Loch Lochy and Loch Linnhe to the west coast.

SIGHTS

Balnain House

Unusual museum of Highland music where visitors can try Scottish instruments, listen to music and sample Scottish specialities.
Tues-Sun 10.00-17.00, July/Aug also Mon; 40 Huntly Street

Flora MacDonald's Monument

There is a fine view of the town and its environs from ◁▷ *Castle Hill* on top of which stands a monument to Flora MacDonald who saved Bonnie Prince Charlie from imprisonment after the Battle of Culloden. The castle itself was built between 1834 and 1846 on the foundations of an old fortress and is now occupied by the local council.
Castle Hill

Loch Ness Video Show

If you want to know more about the legend of the Loch Ness Monster, this documentary sheds light on the endless search for Nessie. There is also an exhibition on kilt making.
Daily 09.30-21.30; 4/9 Huntly Street, Kiltmaker Building

St Andrew's Cathedral

Built in 1866 in the Gothic style. Beautifully polished columns in Peterhead granite. The baptismal font is a copy of the Thorvaldsen font in Copenhagen cathedral.
Daily 09.00-21.00; Ness Walk

MUSEUM

Inverness Museum and Art Gallery

Highland life is illustrated alongside Jacobite memorabilia and bagpipe models.
Mon-Sat 09.00-17.00; Castle Wynd

RESTAURANTS

Dranaway Restaurant and Poolside Brasserie

Good restaurant and bar in the *Craigmonie Hotel*.
9 Annfield Road; Category 2; Tel. 01463 231 649

Glen Mhor Hotel-Restaurant

Top-class Scottish cuisine. Snacks available in *Nico's Bistro*.
10 Ness Bank; Category 2; Tel. 01463 234 308

SHOPPING

As well as the new *Eastgate Shopping Centre*, Inverness has many shops selling woollens, tweeds, tartans and other typical products: eg *Scottish Sweater Store (9 Drummond Street)*; *Duncan Chisholm and Sons Ltd (47-51 Castle Street)*; and, in the southern outskirts, *James Pringle (Holm Woollen Mills)*.

HOTELS

Craigside Lodge

Good view over the town, coast and Loch Ness. Comfortable and friendly atmosphere. Close to the city centre. 6 rooms.
4 Gordon Terrace; Category 3; Tel. 01463 231 576, Fax 713 409

Culloden House Hotel

Bonnie Prince Charlie's headquarters before the Battle of Culloden, the building now houses one of Scotland's finest hotels. Tastefully furnished, good food magnificent gardens. 23 rooms.
Culloden; Category 1; Tel. 01463 790 461, Fax 792 181

Kingsmills Hotel

Country house in beautiful garden with 84 comfortable rooms.
Culcabock Road; Category 1; Tel. 01463 237 166, Fax 225 208

Moyness House

Quiet setting with friendly atmosphere. Good food. 7 rooms.
6 Bruce Gardens; Category 2/3; Tel./Fax 01463 233 836

ENTERTAINMENT

Eden Court Theatre

This modern glass complex, built in 1976, houses a theatre and conference centre. It is used for plays, films, concerts and exhibitions. There is also a good restaurant inside the complex.
Bishop's Road; Tel. 01463 239 841

Folk Singing Club

❂ Every second Sunday at 20.30 in the *Beaufort Hotel (Culduthel Road)* and every evening in the *Market Bar (Market Lane)*.

Scottish Showtime

An entertaining good nightly event for anyone wanting to hear traditional songs and music performed together with Scottish folk dancing.
Mon-Sat from 20.30, early June to end Sept; Cummings Hotel, Church Street

INFORMATION

Tourist Information Centre

Castle Wynd; Tel. 01463 234 353, Fax 710 609

A price on Nessie's head

The Loch Ness Monster has apparently been sighted on more than 3000 occasions in the last 50 years, but proof of its existence is still not forthcoming. So the £500,000 reward offered years ago by Guinness for Nessie's capture is still up.

Aviemore (113/E–F 5)

Strathspey is Britain's largest winter sports resort area and Aviemore is its focal point. Apart from skiing, it is also a good base for walking tours.

Beauly (113/D 3)

A pretty spot by the Beauly Firth with the ruins of a *Cistercian abbey* dating from 1230. ★ *Glen Affric*, one of the most beautiful valleys in Scotland, is within easy reach. Great walking country with river, forest, lochs and mountains.

Cairngorms (113/F 5)

The highest mountain range in Britain with several impressive peaks over 1230 m (3960 ft) high. It is a popular skiing region. A chairlift operates all your round and takes you up to a height of 1097 m (3620 ft) for a ⤱ fine panoramic view.

Caledonian Canal (112/B 5)

The canal runs from Clachnaharry near Inverness to Corpach near Fort William and links the lochs of the Great Glen: Loch Lochy, Loch Oich and Loch Ness. Opened in 1822 to plans by Thomas Telford, this is one of the loveliest waterways in Europe. Small cruisers take passengers along parts of the canal, but it gets crowded during the summer.

Cawdor Castle (113/F 3)

This castle with its tall central tower (1372) has been the home of the Cawdor family (of *Macbeth* fame) for 600 years. According to

The Caledonian Canal runs from east to west through the Great Glen

legend, it was here that King Duncan was murdered. The gardens are spacious and attractive. *May-Oct daily 10.00-17.00*

Culloden Moor (113/E 3)

★ On 16 April 1746, on a moor outside Inverness, Bonnie Prince Charlie's Highland army was defeated by English troops under the leadership of the Duke of Cumberland. The failure of this Jacobite uprising that aimed to restore the Stuart dynasty to the Scottish throne, was a decisive moment in Scottish history. English control over Scotland was never again challenged in battle and the clans lost their autonomy.

The *Battlefield of Culloden* is now a memorial to the Scottish clansmen who died. Visitors can walk freely around the battle site. Flags mark the positions of the two armies and clan graves are marked by headstones: 30 Jacobites were burnt alive outside *Old Leanach Cottage*, now part of the Visitor Centre (*daily 09.00–18.00*).

Dornoch (113/F 2)

This small, attractive coastal town (pop. 900), once the administrative centre of Sutherland county, boasts a fine beach and a 13th-century parish church, formerly a cathedral. *The Royal Dornoch Golf Club* was founded in 1616.

Elgin (114/C 3)

The best feature of this market town (pop. 19,000) is the ruined cathedral, founded in 1224. It was badly damaged by Cromwell's troops in 1650. The west façade and the chapterhouse are particularly striking.
Mon-Sat 09.30-18.30, Sun 14.00-18.30

Fort Augustus (113/D 4)

Once an English fortress, Fort Augustus lies at the south-western end of Loch Ness. Sailors navigating the *Caledonian Canal* often take a break here as they wait for their vessels to pass through the locks. The Benedictine Abbey, built on the site of the original fort in 1876, now houses an interesting heritage centre. The *Clansman Centre* next to the swing bridge is also worth visiting (*daily 10.00-18.30*).

Highland Folk Museum (113/E 5)

Open air museum illustrating the crofters' way of life.
April-Oct Mon-Sat 10.00-18.00, Sun 14.00-18.00, Nov-March Mon-Fri 10.00-15.00; Kingussie

Highland Wildlife Park (113/E 5)

★ Wolves, lynx, eagles, otters, pine martens and shaggy-haired Highland cattle – all the animals that once roamed freely throughout the country, can be seen on this 100-hectare site.
April-May and Sept-Oct daily 10.00-16.00, June-Aug 10.00-17.00; Kincraig

Landmark Visitor Centre (113/F 4)

Informative exhibition recounting the history of the Highlands and its inhabitants. The *Scottish Forestry Heritage Centre* focuses on the importance of timber in the region's history.
April-Oct daily 09.30–18.00 (until 20.00 in July and Aug), winter until 17.00; Carrbridge

Loch Ness (113/D 4)

The most famous and deepest, though not the most beautiful, of the Scottish lochs. Find out everything there is to know about

Nessie at the *Loch Ness Monster Exhibition Centre* in Drumnadrochit (*Daily 09.30-19.30 in summer, 10.00-16.00 in winter*).

Malt Whisky Trail

This 110 km (68,3 mi) long circular tour starts in *Dufftown* (**114/B4**), 'Malt Whisky Capital of the World', and home of the *Glenfiddich Distillery*. This, and other famous distilleries along the trail (like Glenlivet, Tamnavulin, Glenfarclas, Tamdhu, Glen Grant and Stratisla), all offer guided tours.

Mon-Fri normally 09.30-16.30, Sat 10.00-16.00, some are open on Sun. The trail is signposted; brochures are available from BTA.

Urquhart Castle   (**113/D 4**)

Urquhart dates from the 12th century. Once one of the largest castles in Scotland, it was almost completely destroyed by the English in 1692 to prevent the Jacobites from gaining a foothold in this area. On Loch Ness.
Apr-Sept daily 09.30-18.30, low season 09.30-16.30, Sun 11.30-16.30

Urquhart Castle on Loch Ness was one of Scotland's largest castles once

STIRLING

(108/A 5) Not far from Edinburgh and on the main route up to the Highlands, Stirling (pop. 35,000) occupies a strategic location. It has lived through many bloody battles, as English and Scots struggled for ascendancy from as far back as the Middle Ages. The great Scottish heroes, Robert the Bruce and William Wallace, both triumphed over the English army nearby, giving Stirling a special place in the hearts of Scottish nationalists. Stirling Castle was the venue for the coronation of Mary Queen of Scots in 1543, and her baby son, James VI, was crowned in the Church of Holy Rude nearby. It is a bustling town with a good shopping centre and its location makes it an excellent base for exploring the Central Highlands.

SIGHTS

Argyll's Lodging
The founder of the colony of Nova Scotia, Sir William Alexander, built this Renaissance-style town house in 1632. Part of it is used as a youth hostel.
Castle Wynd

Church of Holy Rude
In this 15th-century church, the son of Mary Queen of Scots, James VI, was crowned at just 13 months.
Daily 10.00-17.00, Sunday service at 11.00; St John Street

Guildhall
Sometimes known as Cowane's Hospital, the Guildhall dates from the mid-17th century. It was originally an almshouse for elderly members of the merchant's guild.

Guided tours by appointment, Tel. 01786 462 373 or 479 000; St John Street

Mar's Wark
As you walk up to the castle, you will notice a richly decorated façade at the top of Broad Street. This is all that remains of the palace intended for the Earl of Mar, Regent of Scotland. Begun in 1570, it was never completed.

Stirling Bridge
The old bridge over the Forth lies on the edge of town. Built around 1400, for centuries it was of vital strategic importance, controlling access to the Highlands. The present, rather sad stone bridge was built to replace the wooden one that witnessed William Wallace's victory over the English in 1297.
By the A9 north of the town centre

Stirling Castle
★ It is said that Scotland's history rests on two rocks: the castles of Edinburgh and Stirling. Stirling Castle stands on a basalt outcrop some 75 m (250 ft) high. When it was seized by Edward I in 1297, the hero of Scottish independence, William Wallace, recaptured it. In 1304 it fell back into English hands, but was regained within 10 years when the Scots defeated the English at the Battle of Bannockburn. For several centuries thereafter it was the seat of the Stewarts. Mary Queen of Scots spent her childhood here, as did her son, James VI. *The Great Hall*, which dates from the 16th century, James V's *Renaissance Palace* and the *Chapel Royal* (1594) are among the highlights. ✧ The view that extends as far as the Grampians through *Queen Mary's*

Lookout, a hole in the rampart walls, is breathtaking. Part of the castle houses the *Argyll and Sutherland Highlanders Museum*.
April-Sept daily 09.30-18.00, Oct-March daily 09.30-17.00

MUSEUM

Smith Art Gallery and Museum

History and handicrafts are the focus of this recently modernized museum and art gallery in King's Park. Recent winner of the Scottish Museum of the Year Award, it offers an excellent introduction to the history of Stirling, with a varied programme of events.
Tues-Sat 10.30-17.00, Sun 14.00-17.00

RESTAURANTS

The Barton Bar and Bistro

Smart café-bar serving tasty food.
31/2 Barton Street; Category 3; Tel. 01786 616 98

The Heritage

Small French restaurant.
16 Allen Park; Category 2; Tel. 01786 474 862

The Tolbooth

In the former prison and courtyard. Good food in a warm and friendly atmosphere.
32 St John Street; Category 2/3; Tel. 01786 450 632

SHOPPING

Clan Tartan House

Woollens, tweeds and crafts.
9 King Street

Stewart Campbell Antiques

Antiques, jewellery, art and gifts.
9 and 35 Friars Street

HOTELS

Forth Guest House

Five comfortable rooms in a lovely Georgian town house.
23 Forth Place, Riverside; Category 3; Tel. 01786 471 020, Fax 447 220

Garfield Guest House

Small and friendly. 8 rooms.
12 Victoria Square; Category 3; Tel./Fax 01786 473 730

Park View

Mrs Bell's bed and breakfast in a Victorian house. 4 rooms.
5 Balmoral Place; Category 3; Tel. 01786 471 222

INFORMATION

Tourist Information Centre

41 Dumbarton Road; Tel. 01786 475 019, Fax 471 301

SURROUNDING AREA

Aberfoyle   (107/F 4)

The *Scottish Wool Centre* in Aberfoyle attracts many visitors. Learn about the entire process, from sheep-rearing to weaving cloth. Children's corner, café and shops.
Daily 10.00-18.00; Main Street

Achray Forest Drive   (107/F 4)

★ ⤶ Forest tracks heading to the north of Aberfoyle afford great views of the rugged Trossachs.

Arbroath   (109/E 4)

Arbroath is a pretty fishing port and holiday resort renowned for its Arbroath smokies – haddock smoked over wood-chip fires in the local fishermen's backyards. *Arbroath Abbey* was founded in 1178. In 1320 the Declaration of Independence was signed here by which Robert the Bruce was formally recognized as king of Scotland. The *Abbot's House* nearby survived centuries of neglect and is now a museum (*Mon-Sat 09.30-18.30, Sun 14.00-18.30*).

Bannockburn Heritage Centre (108/A 5)

On 24 June 1314, 6000 Scottish warriors faced 20,000 English soldiers in battle here. Robert the Bruce led his army to a glorious victory and won independence. The battle is reconstructed in an audio-visual presentation.
April-Oct, daily 10.00-17.30

Atholl Country Collection (108/B 3)

This collection of farming tools and other everyday objects gives an insight into the rural life of bygone days.
Mon-Fri 09.30-17.30, Sat/Sun 13.30-17.30; The Old School

Blair Castle (108/B 2)

★ Blair Castle has been the seat of the Duke of Atholl, chief of the Murray clan, since 1629. Its many

A pipe band in front of Blair Castle

famous guests have included Mary Queen of Scots and Bonnie Prince Charlie. Visiting the castle in 1844, Queen Victoria granted the Duke of Atholl the unique privilege of running a private army, known as the Atholl Highlanders. A parade of them still takes place every year (*last Sun in May*). The interior gives a good insight into castle life of the past. Exhibits of weapons, porcelain and furniture.
April-Oct daily 10.00-17.00

Callander (108/A 4)

The *Rob Roy and Trossachs Visitor Centre* provides information on walks in the Trossachs, and the life and times of Robin Hood's Scottish counterpart. Rob Roy's noble deeds were immortalized in Sir Walter Scott's eponymous novel.
Daily 09.30-18.00, July/August 09.00-22.00; Ancaster Square

Cambuskenneth Abbey (108/A 5)

The Augustinian abbey, now in ruins, was built in 1147. The Scottish parliament met here in 1326 under Robert the Bruce.
Mon-Sat 09.30-18.30, Sun 14.00-18.30

Castle Campbell (108/B 5)

♨ Perched on a hill near the town of *Dollar* are the impressive ruins of the 15th-century castle built by the Earl of Argyll and destroyed by Cromwell in 1650. Splendid views of the Forth valley.
Mon-Sat 09.30-18.30, Sun 14.00-18.30

Devil's Elbow (108/C 2)

♨ At 670 m (2210 ft), the lonely *Cairnwell Pass* (A93) is the highest mountain pass in Britain. The tightly winding bends near *Spital of Glenshee* can be dangerous.

Doune Castle (108/A 5)

These romantic, medieval castle ruins date from around the end of the 14th century. They are among the best preserved in Scotland.
Mon-Sat 09.30-18.30, Sun 14.00-18.30

Doune Motor Museum (108/A 5)

The Earl of Moray, owner of Doune Castle, is a car enthusiast. His collection includes the second-oldest Rolls Royce in the world, as well as Jaguars, Aston Martins, Lagondas, Hispano-Suizas and other classic makes.
Mon-Sat 09.30-18.30, Sun 14.00-18.30; near Doune

Dunblane (108/A 5)

An attractive little town (pop. 4500) with a 13th-century cathedral, which was restored at the end of the last century. *The Dean's House* (1624) now houses the *Cathedral Museum* (*June-Sept, Mon-Sat 10.30-12.30 and 14.30-16.30*).

In March 1996, Dunblane came to the world's attention through a terrible tragedy. A lone gunman named Thomas Hamilton walked into the primary school, shot dead 15 children and their teacher, then killed himself.

Dundee (109/D 4)

The seaside town of Dundee (pop. 175,000) makes a good base for excursions in the surrounding area, and has one or two attractions of its own. At *Discovery Point* you can see the restored ship used by Captain Scott in his Antarctic expeditions (*daily 10.00-17.00*). The *Unicorn,* an old frigate with 46 cannons, is moored in *Victoria Dock* (*daily 10.00-17.00*). *Verdant Works* is an old jute mill which has been converted into an interest-ing museum (*daily 10.00-17.00; West Henderson's Wynd*).

Falls of Dochart (108/A 3)

Torrents of water roar through the picturesque village of *Killin,* a good base for walks in the area. The MacNab clan cemetery lies on an island in the River Dochart.

Glamis Castle (109/D 3)

★ The ancestral home of the Bowes-Lyon family who have lived here since 1372, dates from the end of the 17th century. The Queen Mother spent her child-hood here and it is the birthplace of Princess Margaret. It holds a vast collection of antiques and is said to be the most haunted castle in Scotland.
April-Oct daily 10.30-17.30

Highland Motor Heritage Centre (108/C 4)

Veteran cars and costumes in a period setting.
Daily 09.00-17.30; Bankfoot

Huntingtower Castle (108/C 4)

This tower house near Perth was once known as Ruthven Castle. In 1582, young King James VI was lured here in a plot known as the Raid of Ruthven. He was captured by the Earl of Ruthven and held captive for several months.
April-Sept Mon-Sat 09.30-18.00, Sun 14.00-18.00, Oct-March Sat-Weds 09.30-16.30, Sun 14.00-16.30

Meigle Museum (109/D 3)

This small museum has a fascin-ating collection of early Christian carved gravestones and cross-slabs, dating from the 7th to the 10th centuries.
April-Sept Mon-Sat 09.30-18.30, Sun 14.00-18.30

THE CENTRAL HIGHLANDS

Pass of Killiecrankie   (108/B 2)

It was in this gorge in 1689 that 'Bonnie Dundee' and his Highland army put the English army to flight. There is a good network of footpaths to explore in the area.
Visitor Centre: April-Oct daily 10.00-17.30

Perth   (108/C 4)

Scotland's capital until 1452, Perth (pop. 42,000) lies in a picturesque spot by the River Tay. *Perth Art Gallery and Museum (Mon-Sat 10.00-17.00)* has exhibits on local history, art, natural history, archaeology and whisky.

Pitlochry   (108/B 2)

This attractive resort (pop. 2000) is well located for walks and offers plenty of entertainment.

Queen Elizabeth Forest Park   (107/F 4)

★ ⋁⋏ The *Duke's Road* from Aberfoyle to the Trossachs passes through some fantastic scenery. Woods and moorland cover more than 170 sq km (66 sq mi).

Scone Palace   (108/C 4)

Scone Abbey stood on the site of the present residence of the Earl of Mansfield. The Stone of Scone was brought here in the 9th century by Kenneth MacAlpine, and was used as a coronation throne for Scottish kings. In 1296, Edward I seized it and took it to London; it remained there until 1996 when it was returned to Scotland. It is now exhibited in Edinburgh Castle alongside the Honours of Scotland. The old abbey was destroyed during the Reformation. The neo-Gothic palace built in its place is full of priceless antiques and furnishings.
Easter-Oct daily 09.30-17.00

Scotland's Safari Park   (108/A 5)

Sea lions, zebras, elephants, tigers and other exotic animals.
Easter-early Oct daily from 10.00; Blair Drummond

St Andrews   (109/D 5)

The pretty town of St Andrews (pop. 11,000) is the home of golf. Its headquarters are the *Royal and Ancient Golf Club*. The *R & A*, as those in the know call it, houses the *British Golf Museum (May-Oct daily 10.00-17.30; Bruce Embankment)*. The *University*, dating from 1412, is the oldest and most prestigious of Scotland's seats of learning (*guided tours twice daily in summer*). In 1559, during the Reformation, John Knox roused the congregation of the *Cathedral* to such a fever that they plundered it and left it a ruin. ⋁⋏ Climb the 157 steps to the top of *St Rule's Tower* beside the cathedral for a view of the monastic complex, the town and the surrounding countryside.

The Trossachs   (107/F 4)

The small valley of *Loch Achray*, between Loch Katrine and Loch Vennachar, offers a perfect example of the wild and rugged beauty of the Scottish lakes and mountains. The summer season is often quite busy, with lots of people walking in the area and visiting sights. The beautiful forested ravines and gullies can be seen at their best in spring. Sir Walter Scott set his romantic novel *The Lady of the Lake* in the Trossachs and the area became very popular after its publication. The Victorian steamer *SS Walter Scott* cruises the whole length of *Loch Katrine* from Trossachs Pier to Stronachlachar (*April-Sept*).

Glens, lochs and bens

*The west coast, with its islands and inlets,
is regarded by many as the most beautiful corner of Scotland*

The scenery of the Western Highlands is truly magnificent. This wild and rugged region boasts some of Scotland's best-known beauty spots: majestic and sombre Glen Coe; Argyll Forest Park and Loch Fyne; the mountain pass of Rest and be Thankful; and the white sands of Morar between Fort William and the coastal town of Mallaig, especially memorable when seen from the steam train that chugs through this scenic route. On a clear day, the view from Britain's tallest peak, Ben Nevis (1343 m/ 4406 ft), stretches from the west coast with its untidy jumble of offshore islands, as far as the remote Outer Hebrides.

The biggest Hebridean island is Skye, which in Gaelic is called *Eilean Sgiathanach*, meaning the 'winged island', because it juts out from the mainland like a bird's wing. The other islands of the Inner Hebrides can be reached from the small coastal town and popular resort of Oban. Iona is

regarded as the cradle of Scottish Christianity and has become a place of pilgrimage, while on Staffa the incredible Fingal's Cave, a vast cavern lined with basalt columns, is definitely worth a visit if the sea is not too rough. Coll, Tiree and Colonsay all have small hotels and bed and breakfast accommodation. If you are looking for peace and seclusion, any of these three islands will fit the bill. The Isle of Jura offers little in the way of accommodation. Rugged and wild, it is famous for its deer, malt whisky and fine beaches. Eric Blair, alias George Orwell, came to Jura to put his most visionary work, *1984*, to paper.

FORT WILLIAM

(**104/B 6**) The small town of Fort William (pop. 11,000) lies at the heart of the Western Highlands in the shadow of Ben Nevis. Founded in 1655 in honour of William III, it was successfully held by government troops during both Jacobite uprisings. The fort itself was demolished in the 19th century to make way for the

Loch West Tarbert on the island of Harris: bleak and beautiful

railway line, and there is now little in the town centre of historic interest. Fort William's prosperity is largely due to its favourable geographical location and good communication links. It makes an ideal base for excursions to the islands and mountains, and in summer it is a hive of activity filled with coach parties, hill-walkers and families. The north-eastern shores of Loch Linnhe are lined with endless rows of bed & breakfasts and hotels.

SIGHTS

Ben Nevis Distillery Visitor Centre
Small, but informative exhibition in an old whisky distillery, supplemented by a tour of the stills and a whisky sampling session.
Mon-Fri 09.00-19.30, April-Sept also Sat; Lochy Bridge, north of Fort William by the A82

Neptune's Staircase
A flight of eight locks that marks the beginning of the Caledonian Canal, built between 1805 and 1822 (see page 54).
Banavie, north-west of Fort William

MUSEUM

West Highland Museum
Among the varied exhibits are tartans, furniture, weapons, goblets and relics of the Jacobite uprising, including a 'secret' painting of Bonnie Prince Charlie.
Mon-Sat 09.30-18.00, Sun 14.00-17.30; Cameron Square

RESTAURANTS

Crannog Seafood
Good fish restaurant on the shores of pretty Loch Linnhe.
Town Pier; Category 2; Tel. 01397 705 589

MARCO POLO SELECTION: THE WESTERN HIGHLANDS

1 Ardanaiseig Gardens
Delightful gardens and a splendid hotel (page 69)

2 Argyll Forest Park
Nature at its most beautiful (page 69)

3 Outer Hebrides
The last bastion of traditional Highland life (page 67)

4 Colonsay
The remotest island – next stop is Canada (page 69)

5 Dunvegan Castle
The grand seat of the MacLeod clan for over 700 years (page 66)

6 Glen Coe
A bleak and romantic valley, where the notorious massacre of the MacDonald clan was carried out (page 65)

7 Iona
The cradle of Christianity in Scotland (page 71)

8 Skye
Dramatic mountain landscapes on the biggest of the Scottish islands (page 66)

9 Staffa
Small, rocky and uninhabited island featuring Fingal's Cave, one of Scotland's finest natural treasures (page 71)

The Moorings Hotel

Good restaurant, cosy wine bar.
Banavie; Category 2/3; Tel. 01397 727 97

Nevis Range Snowgoose

Self-service restaurant by Aonach Mor skiing complex.
Torlundy; Category 3; Tel. 01397 705 825

SHOPPING

Mairi Macintyre

Offers an excellent selection of stylish clothing and woollens. Good for gifts and souvenirs.
High Street

Peter Maclennan

Caithness glass, crafts, woollens.
28/32, High Street

HOTELS

Alexandra Hotel

Comfortable accommodation in a Victorian building with around 100 rooms.
The Parade; Category 2; Tel. 01397 702 241, Fax 366 677

Inverlochy Castle Hotel

The height of luxury at the foot of Ben Nevis. 17 rooms.
Torlundy; Category 1; Tel. 01397 702 177, Fax 702 953

Lochview Guest House

Great location above the town. 8 comfortable rooms.
Heathercrofft Terrace; Category 3; Tel./Fax 01397 703 149

INFORMATION

Tourist Information Centre

Cameron Square; Tel. 01397 703 781, Fax 705 184

SURROUNDING AREA

Ben Nevis (112/B 6)

Britain's highest mountain rises behind Fort William to a height of 1343 m (4406 ft) and is extremely popular with climbers and hill-walkers. The ascent from Glen Nevis takes about 4 to 5 hours, but the descent is quicker. On a clear day, you can see Northern Ireland from the summit.

Eilean Donan Castle (112/B 3)

Set on a rock in *Loch Duich*, this is one of the most beautiful castles in Scotland. Built in the 13th century, it was destroyed in 1719 and reconstructed between 1932 and 1952. It houses a colourful collection of antiques, weapons and MacRae clan memorabilia.
Easter-Sept daily 10.00-17.30

Glen Coe (112/B 6)

★ It was in this wild and secluded valley in 1692 that the notorious Campbell of Glenlyon, under orders from the English government, carried out the violent and cold-blooded murder of the entire MacDonald clan. *The Glencoe and North Lorn Folk Museum* documents the massacre and the tall, slender cross in the village is a memorial to its victims.
Mon-Sat 10.00-17.30

Glenfinnan Monument (112/B 5)

The memorial column which stands at the head of *Loch Shiel*, crowned with the statue of a Highlander, recalls the landing of Bonnie Prince Charlie in 1745 and the Jacobite uprising which he led. At the *Visitor Centre* you can trace the route he followed with his Highland army.
Daily 09.30-18.00

Old stone bridge on the magical Isle of Skye

Mallaig (112/A 4)

The scenic A830 runs from Fort William to Mallaig at the western end of the North Morar peninsula, opposite the southern tip of Skye. Another memorable trip you can take in summer is along the dramatic Jacobite Steam Railway route, which follows the north shore of Loch Eil. Ferries to Skye depart from Mallaig.

Return journey 5 hours; weekdays 10.35, Sun 12.15

Skye and the Outer Hebrides

★ Skye (**111/D–E 1–4**) is joined to the mainland by a toll bridge from the Kyle of Lochalsh. The *Cuillin Hills* (1000 m/3300 ft) dominate the island, which is 80 km (50 mi) long and 30 km (19 mi) across. *Portree* (pop. 1500) is the capital of Skye, a pretty fishing port on the east side. One of the best places to stay is the *Cuillin Hills Hotel*, renowned for its food, just outside Portree *(25 rooms; Category 2; Tel. 01478 610 03)*. In the south, the restored *Armadale Castle* (**111/E 4**) houses the *Clan MacDonald Centre (open daily 09.30-17.30)*. There are a number of comfortable self-catering cottages in the vicinity.

For over 700 years ★ *Dunvegan Castle* (**119/D 2**) has been the seat of the MacLeod clan chief (*daily 10.00-17.30*). It contains heirlooms, pictures, furniture and letters, as well as the Fairy Flag. According to legend, this scrap of faded silk has magical powers which saved the MacLeod clan from destruction on two occasions. After visiting the castle, take a break in the *Loch Bay Tea Rooms (Category 2/3; Tel. 01470 836 135)* in *Stein* just north of here, where fish and traditional Scottish dishes are served in an old fisherman's cottage. Further north, in *Borreraig* (**119/D 1**), is the *Piping Centre*, a fascinating museum dedicated to bagpipes.

Ferries to the Outer Hebrides leave from *Uig* (**111/E 1**).

The ★ *Outer Hebrides*, also known as the Western Isles (pop. 32,000), are the last bastion of traditional Highland life. *Lewis* (**116–117/C–F 1–5**) is linked to *Harris* in the south by a narrow strip of land. *Stornoway* (**117/E 3**) (pop. 8000), the island capital, is the centre of the Harris Tweed industry and an important fishing port. Ferries to Stornoway leave from Ullapool. The *Nan Eilean Steornoabhagh* museum looks at the history and lives of the local people and the native flora and fauna (*Tues-Sat 14.00-17.00; Town Hall, Point Street*). The *An Lanntair Gallery* (*daily 10.00-17.30; Town Hall, South Beach*) is dedicated to the Gaelic culture and language.

The *Caberfeidh Hotel* (*46 rooms; on the edge of the town, Manor Park; Category 2; Tel. 01851 702 604, Fax 705 572*) offers every home comfort, while the *Seaforth Hotel* (*68 rooms; James Street; Category 2; Tel. 01851 702 740, Fax 703 900*) is more central.

The *Callanish Standing Stones* (**117/D 3**) are thought to date from between 3000 and 1500 BC. Probably a sacred druid site, this stone complex is laid out in the shape of a Celtic cross, with four lanes of monoliths leading into a circle of 13 stones. *Dun Carloway* (**117/D 3**) is another ancient site on the northern shore of East Loch Roag. The *broch*, or circular drystone tower, is Pictish. Nearly 20 m (33 ft) tall, it is one of the best-preserved brochs in Scotland.

The largest village on Harris is *Tarbert* (pop. 300) (**116/C 4**), where the ferry from Skye docks. Accommodation is available in the *Harris Hotel* (*15 rooms; Category 3; Tel. 01859 502 154, Fax 502 281*). At the southern end of the island is the lonely *St Clement's Church* (**116/B–C 5**). The main point of interest here is the tomb (1528) of Alistair Crotach, the 8th MacLeod clan chief. A key is available from the *Rodel Hotel*.

The islands of *North Uist* and *South Uist* (**116/A–B 5–6**) are linked by the bridge and causeway across *Benbecula* (**A2-3**). Further south is the tiny island of *Barra* (pop. 1100) (**0**). The main place of interest here is *Kisimul Castle* which stands on a rock in the middle of Castlebay harbour. For centuries, this was the home of the lawless MacNeil clan. Although it was almost completely destroyed at the end of the 18th century, the castle was restored this century by the 45th clan chief. Ferries travel between Lochboisdale on South Uist and Oban on the mainland.

OBAN

(**107/D 3**) The small coastal town of Oban (pop. 8000) by the Firth of Lorne is protected from the offshore winds by the Inner Hebrides. Oban is the second most important tourist centre in the Western Highlands after Fort William and tends to get quite crowded in summer. Cruises set out from the harbour, and ferries carry passengers, sheep and supplies to the islands.

The town centre is dominated by McCaig's Tower, a replica of the Colosseum in Rome. Oban is an ideal base for tours of the islands, as well as for inland excursions. The town has a varied programme of events in summer and offers many hotels and bed & breakfasts. If you want something more luxurious, try one of the excellent country hotels outside town.

Highland Theatre

Audio-visual presentation of excursions you can take into the mountains and to the islands.
Daily 09.30-22.00; George Street

McCaig's Tower

McCaig's Folly, as the mock Colosseum is also known, dates from the end of the 19th century. It was financed by John McCaig, a 'philanthropic' banker who wanted to erect a monument to himself, while at the same time reducing off-season unemployment. ✥ The views from up here over the coast and islands are stunning.

Oban Distillery

The Oban distillery in the centre of town was founded in 1794. Guided tours are rounded off with a dram of Oban whisky.
Mon-Fri 09.30-17.00; Stafford Street

Gallery Restaurant

Good food. In the town centre.
Argyll Place; Category 3; Tel. 01631 646 41

Manor House Hotel and Green room Restaurant

Excellent restaurant with sea view.
Gallanach Road; Category 2; Tel. 01631 562 087

McCaig's Tower: Rome in Oban

Beechgrove Guest House

Small but elegant hotel in a fine location. 3 rooms.
Croft Road; Category 3; Tel. 01631 566 111

Manor House Hotel

Great view over Oban Bay. Food and comfort beyond reproach. Victorian building with 11 rooms.
Gallanach Road; Category 1; Tel. 01631 562 087, Fax 563 053

Roseneath Guest House

Small hotel in a quiet spot. For non-smokers only. 10 rooms.
Dalriach Road; Category 3; Tel. 01631 562 929

Tourist Information Centre

Boswell House, Argyll Square; Tel. 01631 563 122, Fax 564 273

Ardanaiseig Gardens   (107/E 3)

★ Overlooking *Loch Awe*, one of Scotland's largest and most beautiful lakes, these pretty gardens are planted with rhododendrons, azaleas and rare trees. Nearby is the exclusive 14-room *Ardanaiseig Hotel* (*Kilchrenan, Argyll; Category 1; Tel. 0186 633 33, Fax 632 22*).

Argyll Forest Park   (107/E 4)

★ A beautiful part of the Highlands between Loch Eck, Loch Goil and Loch Long, with plenty of footpaths to explore.

Campbeltown (Kintyre) (106/B-C 5)

This rather unattractive town (pop. 6000) in a remote spot at the southern end of the *Kintyre*

Peninsula is best known for its whisky distillery. A few kilometres further south, beyond the tip of the 'finger', lies the *Mull of Kintyre*. ↘ The view from this landmark is incredible and the journey down the west coast of Kintyre is equally picturesque. Ferries to Arran depart from *Claonaig.*

Castle Stalker   (107/D 2)

This 15th-century castle stands on a small island in *Loch Linnhe*, 25 km (16 mi) north-east of Oban.
Crossing by prior arrangement; Tel. 01631 730 234

Coll   (106/A–B 1)

This flat, bare island and the neighbouring island of *Tiree* can be reached four times a week from Oban via the Isle of Mull. Accommodation is available in the smart *Coll Hotel* (*6 rooms; Tel. 01879 230 334, Fax 230 317*). Until 1750, *Breacachadh Castle* was the seat of the MacLean clan. It is the best example of a medieval castle on the west coast (*by appointment; Tel. 01879 34 44*).

Colonsay   (106/B 3–4)

★ A small, remote island for those in search of total solitude. Lots of plant and birdlife. Three ferries a week sail from Oban. The crossing takes about 2 hours. *Colonsay Hotel* (*10 rooms; Category 3; Tel. 01951 200 316, Fax 200 353*) offers every comfort.

Dunadd Fort   (106/C 4)

On a rocky hill south of Oban and west of the A816 lie the ruins of *Dunadd Fort*, one of Scotland's most important Celtic sites. It was one of the capitals of the ancient Scots kingdom of Dalriada (AD 500-800).

Inveraray Castle: seat of the Duke of Argyll

Dunstaffnage Castle (107/D 2)
Fortified castle north of Oban, near the ruins of a chapel.
April-Sept Mon-Sat 09.30-18.30, Sun 14.00-18.30

Easdale Island
Folk Museum (106/C 3)
An insight into the arduous life of the crofters on Seil and Luing islands in the 19th century.
Mon-Sat 10.30-17.30, Sun 10.30-16.30; Easdale

Eriska (107/D 2)
This tiny island to the north of Oban is renowned for the exclusive *Isle of Eriska Hotel* – a turreted Scottish Baronial mansion that dates from 1884. It is currently part of the Heritage Hotels chain.
Isle of Eriska, Ledaig, near Oban; Category 1; Tel. 01631 720 371, Fax 720 531

Gigha (106/B 5-6)
Off the west coast of the Kintyre Peninsula (*car ferry to Ardminish from Tayinloan*) lies the small, but fertile island of *Gigha* (pop. 200). The warm Gulf Stream air, a total absence of frosts and acid soil together provide perfect conditions for subtropical plants to flourish in *Achamore House Gardens*. They were laid out after World War II by Sir James Horlick, whose fortune was made from the eponymous bedtime drink. Accommodation is available in the *Gigha Hotel*, a comfortable old inn (*13 rooms; Category 2; Tel. 01583 505 254, Fax 505 244*).

Inveraray Castle (107/E 4)
The grand family seat of the Campbells of Argyll, once the most powerful Scottish clan. Work on the present-day castle

began in 1743. It now houses some important art treasures.
April-June and Sept-Oct Mon-Thurs, Sat 10.00-13.00 and 14.00-18.00, Sun 13.00-18.00; July-Aug Mon-Sat 10.00-18.00, Sun 13.00-18.00

Iona (106/A–B 2)
★ In 563, an Irish monk by the name of Columba landed on this small island with 12 followers and founded a monastery that was to become the 'cradle of Christianity' for the British Isles. For centuries, Iona was the last resting place of Scottish kings and clan chiefs, Duncan and Macbeth among them. One of the most recent graves in the abbey is that of John Smith, the former Labour Party leader who died in 1994. The 13th-century buildings, including the *cathedral*, were abandoned after the Reformation. The new cathedral was built at the beginning of this century. *St Oran's Chapel*, which dates from 1080, is the oldest building on the island. Iona can be reached by boat from Oban or via Fionnphort/Mull. Accommodation is available in the pleasant *St Columba Hotel* (*23 rooms; Category 2/3; Tel. 01681 700 304*).

Islay (106/A–B 4–5)
This fertile island (pop. 3800) earns its living from cattle, sheep and its 5 whisky distilleries. It is a pretty place lined with cliffs and sandy beaches and dotted with friendly villages. Golfers can play at the Machrie Golf Course near *Machrie Hotel* (*13 rooms, 14 cottages; Port Ellen; Category 2; Tel. 01496 302 310, Fax 302 404*).

Jura (106/B–C 4–5)
This island, 50 km (31 mi) long, has few inhabitants. A single track runs south from the ferry, while the rest of the island can only be explored on foot. The southern end is dominated by three peaks known as the *Paps of Jura*. It was during his three-year stay on Jura (1946-49) that George Orwell wrote *1984*.

Mull (106/B–C 1–3)
Some 500 of the 2000 inhabitants of Mull (9910 sq km/3826 sq mi) live in *Tobermory*. *Duart Castle* on the east coast, opposite Oban, has been the seat of the MacLean clan since the 13th century. As the MacLean clan were Jacobites, the castle was sacked in 1691 and left in ruins. It was restored in 1911 (*May-Oct daily 10.30-18.00*).

Ferries leave regularly from Oban for Craignure (40 mins). Excursions around the island also leave from Oban.

Staffa (106/B 2)
★ *Fingal's Cave* was discovered on this tiny, uninhabited island in 1772 by the explorer, Sir Joseph Banks. The 'Pearl of the Hebrides' can be visited on foot or by boat. It is a vast cavern ca. 80 m (260 ft) deep and up to 22 m (72 ft) tall in places. Hexagonal columns of basalt of varying heights rise up from the floor like organ pipes. The cave inspired Mendelssohn's *Hebrides Overture*, which is subtitled *Staffa*. Other visitors awestruck by its vast dimensions include Queen Victoria, John Keats and Walter Scott. Wordsworth wrote a poem about it and Turner painted it. For nine months of the year rough seas impede access to Staffa, and the *3 Isles Tour* by boat from Oban sometimes has to be cancelled because the swell is too great to risk.

Remote villages and faraway islands

*The deserted landscapes and Hebridean islands
of the north seem far from civilization*

After the bens, lochs and glens of the Central Highlands, the journey into the far north of Scotland springs many new surprises. It is a world still largely untouched by man, characterized by its unique rugged beauty and sense of isolation. The Grampians, Speyside and Deeside are now so geared for tourism that you do not have to travel far to find a Visitor Centre, a souvenir shop or a castle car park full of coaches. Not so up here. Heading north beyond Gairloch, the signs of civilization become few and far between.

The most scenic stretch of the northbound route is the coast road along the Minch, the channel between the mainland and the Outer Hebrides. Once past the small fishing and ferry port of Ullapool, you will leave urban life behind. The villages signposted consist of no more than a few scattered houses, where the choice of accommodation is limited. You won't find many country mansions with luxury rooms and

The edge of the world: Duncansby Head and Duncansby Stacks

gourmet cuisine. Here the hotels and guest houses are small and modest. But while you may have to forego some of life's luxuries, you will be amply rewarded with an exhilaratingly barren and desolate landscape. For many visitors to Scotland, the drive along the tortuous northern coast roads turns out to be the highlight of their holiday.

It is only a short boat ride from the north-eastern tip to the Orkneys. Like the Outer Hebrides, this remote archipelago has its own special appeal and a history that goes back 4500 years.

ULLAPOOL

(118/A 5) A row of gleaming, low white houses stands out against the dark wall of rocks rising out of the sea. The port of Ullapool (pop. 1000), set on the shores of Loch Broom at the point where it opens out into the sea, is an outpost of civilization in the sparsely populated north. Founded by the British Fisheries Association in 1788, Ullapool is now one of the busiest fishing ports in Britain. During the fishing season, scores of trawlers moor beside the quay and empty their nets into waiting lorries. In the summer, Ullapool turns into a thriving tourist town. Boats cruise along the coast taking passengers over to the islands and on fishing trips. If you are driving, Ullapool lies along the ★ *Wester Ross Coast Road*, one of the most beautiful stretches of road in the Highlands. Car ferries depart from Ullapool for Stornoway on the Isle of Lewis.

MUSEUM

Ullapool Museum
The small collection of exhibits in this municipal museum illustrates the importance of fishing to the local economy.
Mon-Sat 09.00-18.00; Quay Street

RESTAURANT

The Ceilidh Place
Scottish specialities. Good haggis.
14 West Argyll Street; Category 3; Tel. 01854 612 103

HOTELS

Altnaharrie Inn
Exclusive hotel on the banks of Loch Broom with its own ferry service to transport residents to and from Ullapool. First-class cuisine. 8 rooms.
Category 1; Tel. 01854 633 230

Arch Inn
Lovely views over Loch Broom. 12 rooms.
11 West Shore Street; Category 3; Tel. 01854 612 454

The picturesque town of Ullapool thrives on fishing and tourism

MARCO POLO SELECTION:
THE NORTHERN HIGHLANDS

1 Beinn Eighe National Nature Reserve
Pine martens and wildcats, buzzards and golden eagles, and exotic flora (page 75)

2 Cape Wrath
The north-western tip of the British mainland (page 75)

3 Inverewe Gardens
By far the most unusual of Scotland's gardens (page 77)

4 Inverpolly National Nature Reserve
Lessons in wildlife and geology at Knockan Cliff (page 77)

5 Lochinver
An exceptional coastal spot; popular amongst fishing enthusiasts (page 78)

6 Wester Ross Coast Road
Picturesque route along the west coast (page 79)

Four Seasons Travel Lodge
Modern family hotel outside Ullapool with a fine view of Loch Broom. 16 rooms.
Garve Road; Category 3; Tel. 01854 612 905, Fax 612 674

Royal Hotel
A largish, well-run and comfortable hotel with good quality food. 30 rooms.
Garve Road; Category 2; Tel. 01854 612 181

INFORMATION

Tourist Information Centre
West Shore Street; Tel. 01854 612 135

SURROUNDING AREA

Ardvreck Castle (118/B 4)
By the lonely banks of *Loch Assynt* stands the three-storey ruin of the MacLeod chief's castle (1490).

Beinn Eighe National Nature Reserve (112/B 2)
★ Nature trails run deep into this wild and beautiful region south of

Loch Maree. By the southern shores of the loch, near Shatterdale, a signposted walk leads to *Victoria Falls*, named after Queen Victoria who stayed here. The *Aultroy Visitor Centre (open daily in summer, 10.00-17.00)* provides information on the flora and fauna, and brochures on the trails through Britain's oldest wildlife sanctuary.

Ben Hope (118/C 3)
This mountain emerges from an almost primeval landscape in the far north and rises to a height of nearly 1000 m (3300 ft).

Cape Wrath (118/B 2)
★ While the name may seem appropriate given the relentless pounding of the waves in this exposed spot, the word 'wrath' actually derives from the Norse *parph*, meaning 'turning place'. This headland was a key landmark for Viking ships coming to raid the coast. It is the most north-westerly point of Britain and a lighthouse (1828) by the cliffs warns ships away from the treacherous rocks. In summer, a combined

Highland cattle

Highland cattle are just as much a part of this landscape as the bens, glens and lochs. They are highly prized among cattle breeders for their shaggy, golden hair and long horns, as well as for the richly flavoured meat they produce. Despite this, the native species does not seem to be much in favour among local farmers. The cows that graze on the Highland meadows are mainly imported black and white breeds.

ferry and minibus service transports tourists from *Durness* to the Cape (20 km/12½ mi).

Corrieshalloch Gorge (118/A 6)

In this narrow, deep ravine, the *Measach waterfalls* at *Braemore* plunge 50 m (165 ft). The best view is from the suspension bridge.

Dounreay Exhibition Centre (119/E 3)

The prototype fast reactor with its eerie white dome was decommissioned in 1994. Dounreay now processes nuclear waste (*visitor centre and exhibition space open daily*).

Duncansby Head (119/F 3)

Duncansby Head, the eastern counterpart to Cape Wrath, is a steep sandstone promontory crowned with a lighthouse. Just offshore to the south lie the impressive *Duncansby Stacks* – three huge pointed rocks, constantly pummelled by the waves. *John o'Groats* is a short walk from here.

Dunnet Head (119/F 3)

Contrary to popular belief, the northernmost point of mainland Britain is not John o' Groats, but Dunnet Head. ⚐ There is a spectacular view from here of the Pentland Firth to the Orkney Islands and along the coast to Ben Hope. The bay is becoming increasingly popular with surfers.

Dunrobin Castle (119/D 6)

Just north of Golspie, at the end of a tree-lined avenue, stands this fairy-tale castle. It is the ancestral seat of the Sutherland family who were the driving force behind the Highland Clearances – the eviction of thousands of crofters in order to turn the land to pasture. Built in neo-Baronial style between 1845 and 1850, it is often compared to a Loire valley château. With its 150 rooms and beautiful grounds, the castle reflects the wealth of its proprietor, one of the biggest landowners in Europe. It has some fine portraits and two paintings by Canaletto. *Easter and May to mid-Oct Mon-Sat 10.30-17.30, Sun 13.00-17.30*

Durness (118/C 3)

Remote seaside village (pop. 350) on a lofty coast, 20 km (12½ mi) from *Cape Wrath*. Accommodation in bed & breakfast or at the *Parkhill Hotel* (*15 rooms; Category 2/3; Tel. 01971 511 202, Fax 511 321*).

Eas Coul Aulin Falls (118/B 4)

The highest (200 m/660 ft) and most impressive waterfall in the UK is situated at the far end of *Loch Glencoul* near *Kylestrome*, just north of Ullapool. A boat ferries passengers to this magnificent site three times a day.
Mr Moffat, Tel. 01971 583 239

76

Gairloch (112/B 1)

A popular seaside resort with a wide sandy beach. Hotels, bed and breakfasts and self-catering accommodation are plentiful. *Gairloch Heritage Museum* (*April-Oct Mon-Sat 10.00-17.00*) focuses on the life of western Highlanders.

Golspie (119/D 6)

The grey town of Golspie lies on the east coast, north of Dornoch Firth, near *Dunrobin Castle*. The *Stag's Head Hotel* (*5 rooms; Category 2; Tel. 01408 633 245, Fax 634 073*) in the centre is a good base for tours of Caithness and Sutherland.

Handa Island Nature Reserve (118/A 3)

This tiny island is known by ornithologists the world over. Razorbills, guillemots, puffins, kittiwakes and skuas are amongst the many bird species that come here to nest. *By boat from Tarbert, April-Sept; Tel. 01971 502 056*

Inverewe Gardens (112/B 1)

★ This beautiful garden was laid out by Osgood MacKenzie who began to landscape this stretch of coast in 1862. Soil was brought over from Ireland and trees were planted to shelter the land from wind and salt. MacKenzie knew the Gulf Stream kept temperatures high enough for delicate plants to survive, and dotted the terraces, walled gardens and footpaths with exotic species from China, Tasmania, the Himalayas and Sri Lanka. *April to mid-Oct daily 09.30-21.00, end Oct-March 09.30-17.00*

Inverpolly National Nature Reserve (118/A–B 5)

★ The *Knockan Cliff* Information Centre (*end May to mid-Sept Mon-Fri 10.00-17.30*) documents the geohistory of this remote region between Ullapool and Inchnadamph and sheds light on the fascinating range of flora and fauna.

The colourful coast of Handa Island

Reindeer and brown bears in the Northern Highlands

The bedrock of the Northern Highlands consists mainly of gneiss. Thought to be between 1400 million and 2800 million years old, it is the oldest stone in Britain. It is upon this base that the 800-million-year-old peaks of Torridonian sandstone rest. At the end of the last Ice Age, over 11,000 years ago and before the great timber clearances began, the Highlands were covered almost entirely in dense forest. Man arrived in Scotland soon after the ice melted - bones of hunted reindeer, brown bears, polar foxes and lemmings have been found in caves. These animals became extinct long ago, along with the last wolf which was shot in the Findhorn valley in 1743 by a hunter named MacQueen.

John o'Groats (119/F 3)

In the 16th century, a Dutchman by the name of Jan de Groot set up a ferry service from here to the Orkneys and made his fortune. Though it is not strictly the northernmost point in the UK, John o' Groats is a symbolic landmark. There is not a lot to see here apart from souvenir shops and a flagpole that marks the spot where Jan de Groot's house stood. *The John o'Groats House Hotel* (*20 rooms; Category 2; Tel. 01955 611 203, Fax 611 408*) is comfortable. There are nice walks from here to *Duncansby Head* and *Duncansby Stacks*.

Kinlochbervie (118/B 3)

Small, isolated fishing harbour a long way from civilization. *The Old Schoolhouse Restaurant and Guesthouse Hotel* (*6 rooms; Category 2/3; Tel. 01971 521 383*)

Lochinver (118/A 4)

★ Head north from Ullapool on the A894 and then take a left at Inchnadamph to this picturesque port. The ruins of *Ardvreck Castle* are to be found beside the beautiful *Loch Assynt*.

Poolewe (112/B 2)

Poolewe is a tiny, picturesque town on the inlet of *Loch Ewe*, near Inverewe Gardens.

Summer Isles (118/A 5)

Boats leave from Ullapool and Achiltibuie, further north on the peninsula, for this group of off-shore islands. *Tanera Mhor* is the biggest amongst them.

Thurso (119/E 3)

Thurso, once an important fishing port (pop. 10,000), is a sober, grey town. Red Caithness sandstone is still exported from here. Ferries to the Orkneys leave from nearby Scrabster.

Tongue (118/C 3)

A quiet seaside resort (pop. 700) at the southern end of the *Kyle of Tongue*. The Ben Loyal and Ben Hope area and the *Strath Naver Valley* to the east provide excellent walking country. The waters around *Bettyhill*, which lies at the mouth of the River Naver, are rich in salmon. The village *museum* recounts the history of the Highland Clearances – the legacy of Scottish defeat at the Battle of Culloden. Pro-English land-owners were encouraged to rent out their land to sheep farmers, rather than to local crofters. The landlords made more money from sheep farming and in this way the government was able to indirectly penalize the rebellious clansfolk. Some of the crofters emigrated to America, Canada and Australia, while many others were pushed out to coastal villages like Bettyhill.

Torridon   (112/B 2)

The mountain landscape around Loch Maree and Loch Torridon is truly impressive. The crimson sandstone peaks of *Liathach* and *Beinn Eighe* rise to a height of over 1000 m (3300 ft). The *NTS Visitor Centre* (*Mon-Sat 10.00-18.00, Sun 14.00-18.00*) near Torridon has information on the local geology, wildlife and walks.

Wester Ross Coast Road   (112/A 3–C 1)

★ The Highland region to the west of Inverness is called *Wester Ross*. Made up of bare, wind-swept hills, it has an austere, hypnotic beauty. The Wester Ross Coast Road is a very scenic route that runs along the dramatic, cliff-lined coast from the Kyle of Lochalsh, through Plockton, Lochcarron, Applecross and Torridon. At Kinlochewe it becomes the A832 and runs along the banks of Loch Maree to Gairloch, Poolewe, past the Measach Falls and the Corrieshalloch Gorge to Ullapool. 170 km/106 mi.

Wick   (119/F 4)

Caithness Glass, known for its exquisite glassware, has a factory in Wick where visitors can watch the craftsmen at work.
Airport Industrial Estate; Mon-Sat 09.00-17.00, Sun 11.00-17.00

Glossary of geographical terms

Many place names and geographical features derive from Gaelic

aber	river mouth	*goe*	small bay
ach (auch)	field	*how*	burial mound
allt (ault)	stream	*inch (innis)*	island
ard (aird)	hill, mound	*inver*	river mouth
bar	summit	*kyle*	narrow channel
beg (beag)	small	*linn*	waterfall
ben	mountain	*monadh*	hill
blair	plain, moor	*mor (mhor)*	large
broch (brough)	Pictish tower	*ob (oban)*	bay
car	bend, curve	*pit*	town
carn (cairn)	pile of stones	*ross*	peninsula
clunie	meadow	*strath*	broad valley
dubh (dhu)	black, gloomy	*tay (tigh)*	house
dun	hill fort	*tulloch (tully)*	small mound
eilean	island	*uam*	cave
firth	narrow inlet	*uig*	corner
gair (gare)	short	*uisge (uisk)*	water
glen	valley, gorge	*voe*	narrow bay

Stone Age relics and sea bird colonies

Many of the customs and traditions of these northerly island groups can be traced back to their Nordic ancestors

The cluster of islands known as the Orkneys may officially be a part of Scotland, but they are, in every sense, a world apart. Only 18 of the 60 or so islands that make up the archipelago are inhabited. The 19,000 islanders have just 100 sq km (386 sq mi) of land at their disposal, but it is very fertile and they prosper from cattle-farming and agriculture. The islands are scattered with the remains of a distant past. Two of the most significant Stone Age relics in western Europe can be found here: the Neolithic village of Skara Brae and the chambered cairn of Maes Howe. Other ancient ruins include Pictish tombs and traces of Viking settlements; Norsemen arrived here in the 8th century and ruled the Orkneys until the 15th century.

As well as all its prehistoric treasures, Orkney boasts a unique flora and the islands provide ideal nesting grounds for over a million sea birds. The archipelago is also a haven for anglers – there are countless freshwater lochs and many brackish lakes filled with sea trout. Anyone with an interest in the history of the two world wars will be drawn to Scapa Flow. The German Navy was scuttled here in 1919, and in 1939 the battleship *HMS Royal Oak* was sunk by a German U-boat. The wreck is now an official war grave.

The Shetland Islands (pop. 27,000) are about the same distance from Norway as they are from the Scottish mainland (ca. 160 km/99 mi), but that does not mean they are out of reach. Air and sea links have vastly improved in recent years and reaching them is no longer a problem. Of the 100 or so islands, only 15 are inhabited all year round. Most of the inhabitants live on Mainland, the biggest island by far. Lerwick, the capital, lies on the eastern side with its harbour sheltered by the neighbouring island of Bressay.

Like the Orkneys, the Shetlands were once part of the kingdom of Denmark and Norway; in 1468 King Christian I ceded them to the Scottish king as a

The pretty harbour of Lerwick, capital of the Shetland Islands, is full of activity

dowry for Margaret of Denmark, future wife of James III. The Norse heritage is still in evidence in the local culture, language and place names. Many old Viking traditions are still maintained.

Shetland is a paradise for bird-lovers (a pair of binoculars is a must): puffins, gannets and ful-mars nest in the millions on the clifftops, lochs and moors. This is also perfect fishing territory; the coastal waters, lochs and rivers are all well stocked. It is thought that the islands have been the natural habitat for the robust little Shetland pony since the Bronze Age.

KIRKWALL

(120/B 3) Visitors to the capital of the Orkneys (pop. 6000), whose grey, weather-beaten houses stand huddled together, are pleasantly surprised by the magnificent red sandstone cathedral which dominates it. Despite its 850 years, it is as well maintained as any other church in Scotland. There is virtually no industry to speak of in Kirkwall and the local council's administrative duties are limited. Daily life in the town goes on with little fuss or commotion. Roads radiate from Kirkwall all over the island.

Kirkwall: town houses and Kirkwall Hotel overlooking the harbour

MARCO POLO SELECTION: ORKNEYS AND SHETLANDS

1 Maes Howe
The largest burial chamber in Europe (page 85)

2 Ring of Brodgar
Prehistoric stone circle (page 85)

3 Skara Brae
An amazingly well-preserved Stone Age village (page 85)

4 Fair Isle
A resting place for migratory birds in the Atlantic (page 87)

5 Jarlshof
A fascinating excavation site (page 87)

6 Mousa Broch
Pictish residential and defensive tower (page 88)

SIGHTS

Bishop's Palace
The Orkneys were once part of the same bishopric as Hamburg and Bremen across the North Sea. The 13th-century Bishop's Palace stands alongside the cathedral and is also made of red sandstone. The round tower dates from the 16th century.
April-Sept Mon-Sat 09.30-18.30, Sun 14.00-18.30

Earl's Palace
The Earl's Palace, completed in 1607, is one of the finest examples of Renaissance architecture remaining in Scotland.
April-Sept Mon-Sat 09.30-19.00, Sun 14.00-19.00

Highland Park Distillery
One of Scotland's finest malt whiskies is produced here. The *Visitor Centre* is very informative.
Guided tours weekdays 10.00-16.00, in summer also Sat; Holm Road

St Magnus Cathedral
This huge cruciform building, founded in 1137, was built by Earl Rognvald in honour of his murdered uncle, Earl Magnus of Orkney. In 1919, the bones of both these men were unearthed below the columns of the central choir bay. The cathedral is in the late Romanesque style with some early Gothic additions; the decorative work is Anglo-Norman. It is still used for church services.
Mon-Sat 09.00-17.00, Sun 14.00-18.00, Oct-March 09.00-13.00

MUSEUM

Tankerness House
During the 16th century, when Orkney traded with many different countries, its wealthy merchants occupied grand houses such as this one. The architectural style of this fine stone building (1574), with its courtyard and garden, reflects a sense of pride and independence. It now houses a museum documenting the history of the Orkney Islands from prehistoric times right through to the present day. If you intend to explore the archaeological sites of the islands, you should make this museum your first stop.
May-Sept Mon-Sat 10.30-17.00, Sun 14.00-17.00

Scapa Flow was of great strategic importance during both world wars

RESTAURANT

Creel Restaurant
South of Kirkwall, on the island of South Ronaldsay, this restaurant has an excellent reputation. Seafood is the speciality.
St Margaret's Hope; Category 3; Tel. 01856 831 311

SHOPPING

You can pick up some authentic souvenirs travelling around the island. Co-operatives sell woollens, there is a whisky distillery and a goldsmith who makes all kinds of gold and silver jewellery.

HOTELS

Bellavista Guest House
Very pleasant hotel some distance from the town centre. Supper and picnic lunches provided. 5 rooms.
Carness Road; Category 3; Tel. 01856 2306

St Ola Hotel
Friendly, family-run hotel by the harbour. Good service and 6 comfortable rooms.
Harbour Street; Category 2/3; Tel./ Fax 01856 875 090

INFORMATION

Tourist Information Centre
Broad Street; Tel. 01856 872 856, Fax 875 056

SURROUNDING AREA

Blackhammar Cairn   **(120/B 3)**
This pile of stones on the south coast of the island of Rousay, thought to date from around the 3rd millennium BC, is a communal burial chamber divided into seven sections. There are several others like it on the island.

Brough of Birsay   **(120/A 2)**
The rocky island of Birsay can only be reached at low tide.

Ancient relics on this remote and exposed island include a number of Pictish tombs, a Romanesque church and the *Earl's Palace* (17th century), built by the Orkney Earls.

Churchill Barriers (120/B 4)

After the battleship *Royal Oak* was sunk by a German U-boat in World War II, Churchill ordered a concrete causeway to be built in Scapa Flow bay, which now provides access to the southern islands. The *Chapel* on Lamb Holm near the causeway was built by Italian prisoners of war.

Gurness Broch (120/A 3)

About 7 km (4 mi) north of Kirkwall stands this 3 m (16 ft) high Pictish round tower. It dates from the Iron Age but was still inhabited during the Viking occupation.
Daily (except Mon/Tues mornings)

Maes Howe (120/A 3)

★ This Stone Age burial chamber, dating from about 2500 BC, is the most important of its kind in western Europe. It forms a passageway 11 m (36 ft) long and 1.2 m (4 ft) high. The interior walls are made up of huge stone slabs. Important figures, such as priests and kings, were buried here. The inscriptions carved on the slabs were left by Vikings who found and robbed the tomb during the 12th century.
Mon-Sat 09.30-18.00, Sun 14.00-18.00

Papa Westray (120/B 2)

Knap of Howa, near the airfield on Papa Westray island, is claimed by many archaeologists to be the oldest standing house in Europe. It is in remarkable condition, pre-served by a sandstorm that buried it around 5000 years ago.

Ring of Brodgar (120/A 3)

★ Of the original 60 stones, only 27 remain standing, the tallest being almost 5 m (16 ft) high. The ancient stone circle is surrounded by a deep ditch.

Scapa Flow (120/A–B 4)

After World War I, some 70 German ships were interned in the bay. In June 1919, the German sailors opened all the hatches and sunk their vessels. In World War II, a German U-boat managed to enter the bay undetected, past obstacles put in place during WWI, and torpedoed the battleship *Royal Oak* which was stationed here at the British naval base. Some 833 sailors lost their lives in the attack, after which Churchill ordered the construction of special barriers. *Visitor Centre* at the new Lyness ferry terminal.

Skara Brae (120/A 3)

★ This prehistoric village, inhabited between 3200 and 2500 BC, is very well preserved. It is not known why the inhabitants abandoned their dwellings, but they remained untouched for over 4000 years, until 1850. Artefacts found on site are displayed in the custodian's office. Others can be seen in the Royal Museum of Scotland in Edinburgh.
Mon-Sat 09.30-19.00, Sun 14.00-19.00

Standing Stones of Stenness (120/A 3)

Only four of the original 4000-year-old stones are still standing, the tallest being 5 m (16 ft) high. Near *Ring of Brodgar*

Stromness (120/A 3)

Stromness (pop. 1800), the only other town on the Orkney Islands apart from Kirkwall, lies on the west side of Mainland and is the port for ferries to and from Scotland. Now a peaceful and picturesque spot, for centuries it was the main port for the Hudson Bay Company and a base for such famous seafarers as Francis Drake and James Cook. The *Hamnavoe Restaurant* is probably the best place to eat here (*Category 2; Tel. 01856 850 606*). If you wish to stay in town, you can choose between the old *Royal Hotel* (*11 rooms; Category 3; Tel. 01856 850 342*) and the *Ferry Inn* (*17 rooms; Category 3; Tel. 01856 850 280, Fax 851 332*). The *Stromness Museum* displays remains of the German fleet and documents the history of the fishing industry as well as of maritime travel (*Daily, except Tues, 11.00-17.00*).

LERWICK

(121/E 4) The capital of the Shetland islands (pop. 7200) is characterized by its solid, grey stone houses, narrow streets and lively harbour. All the activity generated by Sullom Voe, the biggest oil terminal in Europe, at the north end of Mainland, goes unnoticed in this small, but bustling town.

SIGHTS

Clickhimin Broch
A broch (Pictish tower) from the early Iron Age within the fortifications at Loch Clickhimin. A good place for a stroll.
Mon-Sat 09.30-18.30, Sun 14.00-18.30

Fort Charlotte
This fortress was burnt down in 1672 by the Dutch. Restoration was completed in 1781. ⚐ Fine views over Bressay Sound.

The oil boom has had little impact on the Shetlands' capital, Lerwick

Mon-Sat 09.30-18.00, Sun 14.00-18.00

Town Hall

The colourful 19th-century windows in the Town Hall portray Viking figures. The window roses depict the coats of arms of different towns, including that of Christiania, present-day Oslo.
Mon-Fri 10.00-12.00 and 14.00-16.00

MUSEUM

Shetland Museum

The exhibits provide insight into life on the Shetlands from prehistoric times to the present day.
Mon, Weds and Fri 10.00-19.00, Tues, Thurs and Sat 10.00-17.00; Lower Hillhead

HOTELS

Queens Hotel

Comfortable hotel in a solid stone building by the harbour. 26 rooms.
Commercial Street; Category 2; Tel. 01595 692 826, Fax 694 048

Shetland Hotel

Behind the modern façade of this hotel one finds every imaginable comfort. Heated pool. 64 rooms.
Holmsgarth Road; Category 2; Tel. 01595 695 515, Fax 695 828

Solheim

Small, pleasant guest house in the city centre. 5 rooms.
34 King Harald Street; Category 3; Tel. 01595 695 275

RESTAURANT

Ninian Restaurant

Eat in style in the *Shetland Hotel* restaurant.

Holmsgarth Road; Category 2; Tel. 01595 695 515

ENTERTAINMENT

Posers Nightclub

Open until the early hours.
Grand Hotel, Commercial Street; Tel. 01595 28 26

INFORMATION

Tourist Information Centre

Market Cross; Tel. 01595 693 434, Fax 695 807

SURROUNDING AREA

Bressay Island (121/E 4)

The island opposite Lerwick can be reached by car ferry (15 min). Good walking country, especially if you are looking for solitude.

Fair Isle (O)

★ Isolated island between the Orkneys and the Shetlands. A stopping place for migratory birds. Hostel and birdwatching centre.
Ferries Tues, Thurs and Sat from Sumburgh, every other Thurs from Lerwick

Fetlar (121/F 2)

Part of this island in the far northeast is a bird reserve. Accommodation in hired tents.

Foula (O)

Foula's high cliffs provide an ideal breeding ground for sea birds.
Mail boat sails 2 to 3 times a week from Walls; flights from Tingwall

Jarlshof (121/E 6)

★ Traces of settlements covering 3000 years of occupation from the Stone Age through the Viking era to the 17th century.

April-Sept Mon-Sat 09.30-18.30, Sun 14.00-18.30; near Sumburgh airport on Mainland

Mousa Broch (121/E 5)

★ Scotland's most impressive broch (Pictish tower) stands on the island of Mousa. It is 12 m (40 ft) high and 15 m (50 ft) in diameter.
Crossing from Sandwick

Ness of Burgi (121/E 6)

Fortified Stone Age complex at the end of Mainland.

Noss Nature Reserve (121/E–F 4)

Thousands of auks, gannets and gulls nest in the high crevices of this bird sanctuary.
Enquire at Lerwick Tourist Office about crossings from Bressay

St Ninian's Isle (121/E 5)

Among the remains of the early Christian church found beneath the ruins of a 12th-century chapel was a Celtic silver hoard. *St Ninian's Treasure is in Edinburgh (National Museum of Antiquities), but the Shetland Museum in Lerwick has replicas. The island is linked to the Mainland by a strip of sand.

Scalloway Castle (121/E 4)

Scalloway is Shetland's second town. The castle was built by the notorious Earl Patrick Stewart in

1600. When he was executed in 1615, the property fell to ruin.

Shetland Croft House Museum (121/E 5)

This thatched cottage (1860) with original furnishings and outbuildings, illustrates how the Shetland crofters lived and worked.
Daily 10.00-13.00 and 14.00-17.00; Dunrossness, Voe, south of Lerwick

Sullom Voe (121/E 3)

Europe's biggest oil terminal, producing more than one million tons of crude oil daily. North of Brae, by Sullom Voe sound.

Whalsay (121/E–F 3)

The 1000 inhabitants of this small island, east of Mainland, live mainly from fishing and fish processing. *Pier House*, across from Symbister Harbour is one of the two warehouses built for Hanseatic traders who exchanged salt, tobacco, spirits and cloth for Whalsay's dried fish.
Car ferry from Laxo or flight from Tingwall by Loganair

Yell (121/E 2–3)

Old Haa in *Burravoe,* said to be the oldest building on the island, houses an exhibition on the fauna, flora and handicrafts of the island.
Daily (exc Mon, Thurs) 10.00-16.00

In the Marco Polo Spirit

Marco Polo was the first true world traveller. He travelled with peaceful intentions forging links between the East and the West. His aim was to discover the world, and explore different cultures and environments without changing or disrupting them. He is an excellent role model for the 20th-century traveller. Wherever we travel we should show respect for other peoples and the natural world.

From Proud Castles to Rugged Open Spaces

*These routes are marked in green on the map inside front flap
and in the road atlas beginning on page 102*

① SCOTLAND IN MINIATURE: ABBEYS IN THE BORDER LANDS

 Whoever thinks that the real Scotland begins a day's trip north of Edinburgh should make sure to experience the area known as The Borders. There are several destinations south of Edinburgh worth a visit, such as the romantic abbeys and towns of Melrose, Kelso and Jedburgh which date back to the thirteenth century, and Abbotsford House, the former residence of Sir Walter Scott. Our route follows the Teviotdale to the 'Wedding Paradise' of Gretna Green and continues via Dumfries into Burns Country, the home of the Scottish national poet. After reaching the coast near Stranraer, we proceed along the sea to Alloway and the house where Robert Burns was born. A trip around the island Arran is also highly recommended. From there it's not far to Glasgow, where we finish with a sight-seeing tour. The entire drive is about 650 km (404 mi) long, and requires 4 to 5 days.

We leave Edinburgh by proceeding south on the A702 for 11 km (7 miles). Turning left after Penicuik, we come to the famous *Rosslyn Chapel* from the 15th century (page 40) with its rich statuary.

The A703 takes us further to Innerleithen (page 41); south of this little town we come to the ancient *Traquair House* (page 41). Proceeding via Galashiels, we continue on to *Melrose* (page 40) with its romantic abbey ruin in which the heart of Robert the Bruce is said to be buried. 5 km (3 mi) to the west of this town, we visit *Abbotsford House* (page 39), which was commissioned by the writer Sir Walter Scott. From Melrose, it's just a stone's throw to *Dryburgh Abbey* (Scott's final resting-place, page 39). The town of *Kelso* (page 40), found 16 km (10 mi) to the east, is one of the most beautiful in the Borders. The ruined but highly picturesque church tower is all that remains of the abbey here. A splendid view of enchanting *Floors Castle* (tours are available) may be had from the bridge in Kelso. This castle was constructed in 1721 according to plans by William Adam. Our next stop is *Jedburgh* (page 39), with its imposing monastery church ruins. From here we proceed through the beautiful Teviot valley in a southeasterly direction, perhaps stopping for a quick wedding in *Gretna Green* (page 35) at the Scottish-English border. A roundabout route on the coast then brings us to *Caerlaverock Castle* (page 34) before we reach *Dumfries* (page 33) on our pilgrimage to the places that commemorate Robert Burns. Next, we refine our taste buds with a *pint of ale* or *lager* at the Globe Inn, one of the poet's favourite haunts. For artistic enjoyment of another kind, the *Glenkiln Reservoir* (page 35) is not far from Dumfries. (Information is available at the Tourist Office in Dumfries.)

The lovely name *Sweetheart Abbey* (page 35) lures us out of Dumfries in a southerly direction on the D710. After touring the abbey, it's worth making a detour on the coastal road in order to reach Castle Douglas, where we can visit the monstrous *Threave Castle* and the beautiful *Threave Gardens* (page 35). After this, we can drive the couple of miles south off the A75 to the quaint town of *Kircudbright*, in order to see both *Broughton House*, former residence of the painter Edward Atkinson Hornel (1864-1933), and *MacLellan's Castle* (1582). Further along on the A75, we pass the handsome little town *Gatehouse of Fleet*, where The Mill on the Fleet (in an old spinning mill) can be viewed. Right after Gatehouse of Fleet comes the 15th- century *Cardoness Castle* with its beautiful view. Our next turnoff is in the idyllic area near Newton Stewart. We head north on the A714 here to reach *Galloway Forest Park* (page 34), which in its grand solitude is no different from the 'real' highlands. One should leave the car at *Loch Trool* (page 34), and go for a hike (the Loch Trool Forest Trail takes 3 to 4 hours).

The main street A75 brings us to *Stranraer;* this small, rather unattractive beach town is also a harbour for ferries to Belfast. Seven kilometres (4½ miles) before Stranraer on the A75, we come to the tower ruins and beautiful French-influenced gardens of *Castle Kennedy*. Leaving Stanraer, we follow the A77 along the coast to *Girvan*. (Passage to the birdlover's island of Ailsa Craig can be made from here. A round trip takes about 4 to 6 hours; information is available from the Tourist Information Centre.)

The next stop, *Turnberry*, is well known among golfers; main attractions are the luxurious Turnberry Hotel and the world-famous 'greens'. From here it's only a few kilometres to the north-east on the A77 to *Kirkoswald* and *Souter Johnnie's Cottage* (page 45), while the other attraction, *Culzean Castle* (page 45), is located on the coastal road 719 north of Turnberry. Next come the Burns pilgrimage sites of *Ayr* and *Alloway* (page 44), followed by *Ardrossan*, where it's possible to ferry across to the *island of Arran* before we reach the outskirts of *Glasgow* (page 41) via Paisley.

② INTO THE WORLD OF THE CLANS: SUMMER HOLIDAYS FIT FOR A KING

 This tour begins in Edinburgh; it is about 880 km (550 mi) long and takes about 8 days. We drive via Stirling and the Trossachs into the extensive Grampian Mountains. Large cities are not to be found here, while small towns such as Pitlochry, Kingussie or Aviemore are sustained by tourism. The tour continues into the Strath (valley) Spey, where it is possible to visit various famous whiskey distilleries. As we continue in the direction of Aberdeen, we partially follow the Castle Trail with its splendid

examples of old fortresses. Proceeding westward from Aberdeen, we enter the royal summer holiday area, the Dee valley with Balmoral Castle and Braemar. Glen Shee, which runs south towards Dundee, also offers impressive scenery. Our way back to Edinburgh takes us past the golfer's Mecca of St Andrews and Kirkcaldy.

Starting in Edinburgh, we take the toll road A90 in the direction of Forth Bridges; after traversing this town we turn left onto the A985 in the direction of Kincardine. A side trip to *Culross* (page 39) can be made along the way. From Kincardine we take the M9, which we then leave 3.2 km (2 mi) before Stirling in order to visit the *Bannockburn Heritage Centre* (page 59); *Stirling* itself is another destination worth seeing. Following the A84, we come to *Doune* (page 59) and then *Callander* (page 60), the latter being the starting point of an excursion on the A873 and A821 through the wildly romantic area called the *Trossachs* (page 61). The A84 leads further in a northerly direction into the stately remoteness of the mountains and lochs. We drive past Loch Earn and the village of Killin with its *Falls of Dochart* (page 60), then follow the northern shore of Loch Tay for about 25 km (15½ miles). *Castle Menzies,* which lies 2.5 km (1½ mi) northwest of the attractively located town of Aberfeldy, is worth seeing. In Ballinluig we join the A9, which we follow via *Pitlochry* (page 61) and the *Pass of Killicrankie* (page 60), where a magnificent section of road branches off in a westerly direction towards Loch Tummel and Loch Rannoch as well as *Blair Castle* (page 59).

There are no settlements worth mentioning for more than 50 km (31 mi), until you come to the Spey valley near Kingussie (which is home to the *Highland Folk Museum,* page 55). Proceeding via *Kincraig* (page 55), we reach *Aviemore* (page 54). Because of the view, one should not miss the Cairngorm chairlift. The 'Kingdom of Malt Whiskey' begins in Grantown-on-Spey; famous distilleries along the *Malt Whiskey Trail* invite us to stop in for a visit. The A939/A944 leads towards Aberdeen via *Tomintoul* (page 51). Along the way, we can visit the imposing 13th-century ruins of *Kildrummy Castle,* and also make a detour to *Leith Hall* (page 51) and Huntly, where we can visit *Huntly Castle* (page 51). Much-photographed *Craigievar Castle* (page 51) stands south of How of Alford. In fact, the whole area around *Aberdeen* (page 48) is a genuine paradise for castle lovers. One can get the 'Castle Trail' pamphlet at the tourist information office. After a side trip to *Dunnottar Castle* (page 51) south of Aberdeen, we follow the A93 in a southerly direction through the beautiful Dee valley, which is home to *Balmoral Castle* (page 50) and *Braemar* (page 50). Logically enough, this area is full of tourists in summer! Travelling through Glen Shee, the grandeur of the natural beauty of the Highlands is evident in the pass known as *Devil's Elbow* (page 59). We stop again for a tour of *Glamis Castle* (page 60), before coming to the mild coastal region of *Dundee* (page 60). And perhaps one fancies playing a round of golf in *St Andrews* (page 61) before returning to Edinburgh via Kirkcaldy?

③ ADVENTURE IN THE HIGH NORTH: CASTLES, ISLANDS, UNTAMED COASTS

 Our starting point is Glasgow, which has long ago outgrown its former reputation of ugly industrial city. Scottish natural beauty of the finest sort begins just a few miles to the north: Loch Lomond, the Heights of Argyll, and then the Grampian Mountains with the summit of Ben Nevis (1343 m / 4406 ft) near Fort William. After swerving off to Loch Ness, the route continues westward to the splendid island of Skye. From there it follows the dramatically beautiful coastline from Wester Ross and the northernmost highland up to Durness, and continues along the north coast to Cape Duncansby Head. A car ferry from Scrabster takes us to the Orkneys. Taking the coastal road from Wick, we descend via Dornoch to Inverness. In total, the route is about 750 km (466 mi) in length, and takes about 10 days. Lovers of vast solitary spaces and wind-swept countryside will be well served by this tour.

In point of fact, the A82 runs directly from Glasgow to Fort William. But one should take time for this northerly voyage: both the soft allure of *Loch Lomond* (page 45) and the raw beauty of *Glen Coe* (page 65) can best be appreciated in an unhurried fashion. After one's arrival in *Fort William,* a single look into the heavens is sufficient to determine whether the time is right to climb *Ben Nevis* (page 65). A certain amount of (amusing) hustle and bustle will attend our visit to Drumnadrochit at *Loch Ness* (page 55), since Nessie may reappear at any moment. The A887 or Road to the Isles is splendid, bringing us from Loch Ness to the *Isle of Skye* (page 66). A trip around the perimeter of the island is an absolute must! From here we take the *Wester Ross Coast Road* (page 79) heading north via *Gairloch* (page 77), *Inverewe Gardens* (page 77) and *Ullapool* (page 73). The attractive stretch of road which goes to Lochinver, Achmelvich and Drumbeg is almost unknown to non-locals. Bird fans can ferry across to the island of *Handa* (page 77) from either Scourie or Tarbet. In *Durness* (page 76), a visit to *Cape Wrath* (the north-westernmost point of Scotland, page 75) is a highly recommended experience, especially for nature lovers. From Durness, we follow the A836 to *Tongue* and *Thurso* (both page 78); near the latter, car ferries set sail from Scrabster to the *Orkneys* (page 81). Those who have enough time should not miss a side trip to the Orkneys, nor to *Dunnet Head* (page 76), *Duncansby Head* (page 76), and *John o' Groats* (page 76). From Wick, the coastal road A9 runs in a southerly direction. Scotland's high north shows its softer side here: since the east coast is protected from Atlantic storms, *Dunrobin Castle* (page 76) was commissioned as the dream house of a 19th-century nabob. We continue on to *Dornoch* (page 55), have a look at the handsome small town and – if we are thus inclined – make a cameo appearance on the 'green' at the golf club.

Inverness (page 52), the final point of our route, is both the centre of Highland tourism and a good home base for day trips into the surrounding area. The nearby *Culloden Moor* (page 55) is one of the most popular Scottish tourist destinations.

Practical information

Useful addresses and information for your visit to Scotland

ANIMALS

The whole of Great Britain is free of rabies; all animals entering the country are subject to a six-month quarantine as a result. Attempts to circumvent this law are dealt with harshly.

BANKS

Banking hours are usually *Mon through Fri 09.30 to 16.00 or 16.30*. On *Thursdays* many banks extend their opening hours to *17.45*.

BUSES

Although slower than the train, travelling by bus is much cheaper. The two main intercity operators are *National Express* and *Scottish Citylink* (*Tel. 0990 898 989*). Young people under 25, students and senior citizens can obtain a *Discount Coach Card* (£8) which gives 30% off standard fares. The *Tourist Trail Pass* is worth investing in if you don't have a car and wish to travel around. These passes are available for 2 days (adults £49, children aged 5-15 £39), 7 days (adults £120, children £94) and 14 days (adults £187, children £143). They allow unlimited travel on *National Express* and *Citylink* coaches.

There is also a postbus network that operates in rural areas. Time-tables are available from: *Postbus Controller, Royal Mail, 7 Strothers Lane, Inverness IV1 1AA; Tel. 04163 256 273.* For backpackers there are special offers from *Go Blue Banana, Haggis Backpackers* and *Macbackpackers*. Further information can be found in the BTA brochure *Getting About Britain*.

CAMPING

Most campsites are designed to cater for caravans and mobile homes and many people hire camper vans. Bear in mind that the roads in Scotland are often narrow and winding and not ideal for towed caravans. It is possible in places to camp on unofficial ground, but you should get permission from the landowner first.

CLIMBING & WALKING

Scotland's diverse landscape includes a vast range of routes for walkers and climbers, from gentle Sunday strolls to serious hikes. Devoted hill-walkers spend their weekends on the Munros: some 280 peaks which exceed 910 m (3000 ft), listed by Sir Hugh Munro in 1891. Whatever sort of excursion you are planning, there are a few basic guidelines you should follow. Always check the forecast; weather conditions in the hills can change quickly and dramatically so be sure to keep an eye on the sky. Plan your route carefully, taking into account the hazards of the terrain, from peat bogs to rocky outcrops and screes. Tell someone where you are going and when you expect to return. A note left on the windscreen of your car before heading out is always a good idea. Take appropriate clothing and equipment: proper walking boots, waterproofs and enough food and water. A torch, a first aid kit, a whistle and a survival bag can come in useful. Always carry a map, ideally an Ordnance Survey map. Don't attempt hikes and climbs beyond your ability, especially not on your own.

CONSULATES

American Consulate General Edinburgh
3 Regent Terrace,
Edinburgh,
Scotland EH7 5 BW
Tel. 0131 556 8315
Fax 0131 557 6023

Consulate of Canada
3 George Street,
Edinburgh,
Scotland EH2 2XZ
Tel. 0131 220 4333
Fax 0131 245 6010

CUSTOMS

Toll-free importation into Great Britain: 1 litre of alcohol over 22 per cent or 2 litres under 22 per cent, 200 cigarettes or 100 cigarillos or 50 cigars or 250 grams of loose tobacco, 50 grams of perfume or 250 grams of eau de toilette and other articles up to a total value of 145 English pounds.

Toll-free importation into Canada: 200 cigarettes, 50 cigars, 400 grams of loose tobacco, 1 bottle (1.1 litre) of spirits or wine, or 24 bottles or cans (335 ml) of beer or ale, gifts to the value of C$60 per gift, a small amount of perfume for personal use.

Toll-free importation into the USA: 200 cigarettes or 50 cigars or 2 kilograms of tobacco as well as 1.1 litres of spirits. In addition, presents with a total value of $100. The importation of plants, meat, fruit and other fresh foodstuffs is prohibited.

DISABILITY

The Scottish Tourist Board publishes a booklet entitled *Accessible Scotland*, and *Disability Scotland* (*Princes House, 5 Shandwick Place, Edinburgh EH2 4RG; Tel. 0131 229 8632, Fax 229 5168*) keeps a comprehensive database with up-to-date information.

DOCTORS

Tourists from the EU are admitted, in case of emergency, and treated free of charge to hospitals of the *National Health Service (NHS);* American and Canadian tourists should find out whether their health coverage extends to

Europe. If not, it is advisable to purchase travel insurance that will cover medical emergencies.

DRIVING

Driving on the left requires special awareness. Be aware of streets with the right of way, stop signs and traffic circles. Narrow single-lane roads are common in the countryside, particularly in the north-west. They all have clearly marked passing places. The general rule is that the driver nearest the passing place should pull over and allow oncoming traffic to pass. If you are travelling slowly, pull in and let faster traffic behind overtake. They are not meant for parking.

Speed limits: 50 km/h (30 mph) in built-up areas, 95 km/h (60 mph) on other roads and 110 km/h (70 mph) on motorways and dual carriageways.

Documents: insurance documents, drivers licence and registration papers.

Breakdown service: Toll-free emergency numbers which may also be used by non-members: AA (*British Automobile Association*), *Tel. 01256 20123*, and RAC (*Royal Automobile Club*), *Tel. 0181 686 2525*.

Parking in the street: double yellow solid line means stopping is prohibited *Mon–Sat 08.00–18.00*.

ELECTRICAL CURRENT

240-volt alternating current. Travellers from the USA and Canada are strongly advised to acquire an adapter at home if they want to use their hairdryers and electrical razors here — provided, of course, that these appliances are switchable to 240 volts!

EMERGENCIES

To contact the police, fire brigade, ambulance, mountain rescue or coastguard, dial 999.

FERRIES

Apart from the service from Aberdeen to Bergen in Norway and to Northern Ireland from Cairnryan and Stranraer, there are no direct international ferry services to Scotland. Most inter-island services are operated by *Caledonian MacBrayne.* Fares are not cheap, but there are special offers for those on tours and for frequent users. Further details: *Caledonian MacBrayne Ltd, Ferry Terminal, Gourock, Renfrewshire PA 19 1QP; Tel. 01475 650 100.* For P&O services to Orkney and Shetland from Aberdeen and Scrabster contact *P&O Scottish Ferries, PO Box 5, Jamieson's Quay, Aberdeen AB11 5NP; Tel. 01224 572 615.*

INFORMATION

Scottish Tourist Board
PO Box 705, Edinburgh EH4 3EU Tel. 0131 332 2433; Fax 0131 459 2434; e-mail: ww.holiday.scotland.net

British Tourist Authority (BTA)
http://www.visitbritain.com

BTA USA (Chicago)
625 North Michigan Avenue, Suite 1510, Chicago IL 60611 (personal callers only) Toll free: 1-800 462-2748

BTA USA (New York)
7th Floor, 551 Fifth Avenue, New York, NY 10176-0799 Tel. (212) 986-2200 Toll free: 1-800 GO 2 BRITAIN

BTA Canada (Ontario)

5915 Airport Road,
Suite 120,
Mississauga
Ontario L4V 1T1
Tel. (905) 405 1840
Toll free: 1-888 VISIT UK
Fax (905) 405 1835
Addresses for the local Tourist Information Centres are given in the relevant sections of this guide.

OPENING TIMES

Most shops are open from 09.00 until 17.30 or 16.00. Longer opening, times until 19.30 or 20.00, are only found in large cities. Pubs are generally open from 17.00 until 23.00, though some are open all night.

PASSPORTS & VISAS

A passport is sufficient for entry into the UK.

POST & TELEPHONE

Post office opening times: Mon-Fri 09.00-17.30, Sat 9.00-12.30. Normal charges in telephone booths in hotels; mostly direct dialling. Cheaper times 20.00-08.00.
Country code to Canada and to the USA: 001. Country code to Scotland: 0044.
The '0' preceding Scottish area codes should be dropped when dialling from outside the country.

RAILWAY

The railway services offer a number of packages: for the whole of Scotland, for parts and necessary connections. Further information from *BritRail International,* *Tel. 1-800 677-8585.*

SIGHTS

Note that between October and March many sights are closed altogether or have different opening hours. The *Great British Heritage Pass* (valid either 7 days, 15 days, or one month) admits you to more than 120 sights in Scotland alone and many more in the rest of the U.K. Members of the organization *Historic Scotland* are also entitled to free admission as well as other discounts at about 300 selected sights. Info: *Historic Scotland, Salisbury Place, Edinburgh EH9 1SH, Tel. 0131 668 8800*

SPORTS

Cycling

The borders are ideal for cycling tours – other regions of Scotland too. Tour suggestions, addresses of cycling holiday organizers and much more can be found on the map 'Cycling Holidays in Great Britain' which can be obtained from the BTA. The 'Cyclists Touring Club' (CTC) publishes, amongst others, a brochure with the title: 'Cycle-A-Way,' which lists all marked routes. *CTC, 69 Meadow, Godalming, Surrey GU7 3HS. Tel. 1483 417217, Fax 426994*

Fishing

The rivers Spey, Tweed, Tay and Dee are all excellent for salmon fishing. Though popular, it is not a cheap sport and you can pay as much as £1000 for a rod licence for only a few days. There are cheaper places to fish in public waters, but you still have to obtain a licence, available at all fishing shops and post offices.

Fly-fishing is another very popular pursuit in Scotland. If

you have no experience, instructions on how to cast properly are essential. Other types of fishing practised here include dapping – good for catching fish in windy conditions on lochs – and nymph fishing, for which one uses an imitation of a fly larvae. Dry fly-fishing is good on warm evenings on the loch.

Golf

With over 450 courses all across Scotland, there are more places per head for golfing than in any other country in the world. Most courses are open to the general public and green fees are low. Any self-respecting golfer will jump at the opportunity of playing at one of the top courses, such as St Andrews, Carnoustie, Muirfield, Turnberry, Royal Dornoch, Royal Troon or Gleneagles. The hotels and guest houses in the vicinity of the courses offer good golfing packages.

Hiking

Scotland is a hiking paradise for walkers of all levels. Suitable shoes and rainwear are a must. The STB brochure 'Walk Scotland' offers suggestions. The best maps are the *Ordnance Survey Maps* which are offered in a scale of 1:50,000 and "Pathfinder Maps" in a scale of 1:25,000. Even with well sign-posted hiking trails or hiking books a good map is always useful. Some books have extracts from the Ordnance Maps. Addresses of hiking holiday organizers can be found in the BTA brochure 'Hiking in Great Britain'.

Riding

The best region for horse-riding is the Borders. Many of the small border towns have riding centres, some of which also offer accommodation as well as courses for beginners.

Skiing

There are a number of ski centres in the Highlands with a choice of excellent runs. They all hire equipment and offer lessons. The slopes can be icy and pitted with bare patches of rocks, and the wind may be cold and biting, but the setting is stunning.

Swimming

The west coast has a milder climate than the east coast thanks to the Gulf Stream. The most important swimming areas are located here. The water temperature reaches 18 C (64 F) only in sheltered bays. The new recreation centres with wave pools, water slides and solariums, e.g. in Ayr, Dunbaror, and Aberdeen, are dependent on the weather and the season. There are wonderful lonely beaches on the north-west coast, where swimming is only recommended for the hardy types. The water in the very deep Lochs hardly warms up to a comfortable swimming temperature.

Water sports:
Boating, Sailing, Surfing

Travel the canals in a house-boat. Information on this and other types of holiday can be found in the brochure 'Waterfront Britain', *P.O. Box 2644, Broadstone, Dorset BH18 9YT. Fax 01202 243243.*

The Scottish west coast is a popular sailing area. Popular meeting point: Rothesay Bay, Isle of Bute. Boat charter. The organization *Sail Scotland, 7 Alexandra Parade, Dunoon, Argyll PA23 8AB,*

Tel. 01369 705533, Fax 70 55 88, provides information about costs, chartering, sailing schools etc.

TIME

Greenwich Mean Time is used here. Scotland is thus one hour behind Central European Time (CET), except in March (when Central Europe hasn't yet changed to daylight saving time) and October (when Great Britain has already made the switch to standard time). Local time is always applicable for ferries and air travel.

WHEN TO GO

The best time to tour Scotland is during the months of May, June and September. During the high season, July and August, the roads in the Highlands can become very congested.

YOUTH HOSTELS

There are good youth hostels in Scotland. For a full list contact: *Scottish Youth Hostel Association, 7 Glebe Crescent, Stirling FK8 27A; Tel. 01786 891 400, Fax 891 333.* YHA membership is required.

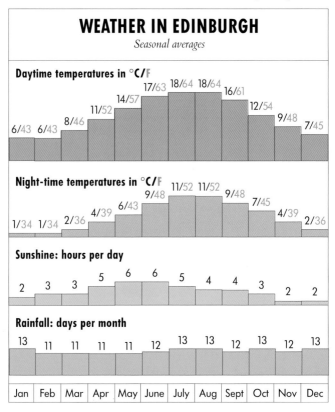

WEATHER IN EDINBURGH
Seasonal averages

Daytime temperatures in °C/F

Jan	Feb	Mar	Apr	May	June	July	Aug	Sept	Oct	Nov	Dec
6/43	6/43	8/46	11/52	14/57	17/63	18/64	18/64	16/61	12/54	9/48	7/45

Night-time temperatures in °C/F

Jan	Feb	Mar	Apr	May	June	July	Aug	Sept	Oct	Nov	Dec
1/34	1/34	2/36	4/39	6/43	9/48	11/52	11/52	9/48	7/45	4/39	2/36

Sunshine: hours per day

Jan	Feb	Mar	Apr	May	June	July	Aug	Sept	Oct	Nov	Dec
2	3	3	5	6	6	5	4	4	3	2	2

Rainfall: days per month

Jan	Feb	Mar	Apr	May	June	July	Aug	Sept	Oct	Nov	Dec
13	11	11	11	11	12	13	13	12	13	12	13

Do's and don'ts

*How to avoid some of the pitfalls
that face the unwary traveller*

Country Roads

Scottish roads, especially in the Highlands, are often narrow and winding. The single-track country roads have passing places here and there to allow cars travelling in opposite directions to pass each other, and to enable faster traffic stuck behind a slow vehicle to overtake. It is strictly forbidden to use these passing places as a car park.

Edinburgh Festival

This is one of the most popular cultural events in Europe and from mid-August to early September, the streets of Edinburgh are packed. If you plan to be in the city for the event, be sure to book your accommodation well in advance. It is definitely worth experiencing the exuberant and convivial atmosphere of this wonderful city during the festival; however, you may find it easier to stay outside Edinburgh and just drive in to catch the shows you are most interested in seeing.

Marshland, moorland and rocks

When exploring the Highlands on foot, do not be tempted to stray from the signposted paths. Marshland, shallow pools and rocky scree all pose dangers to the ill-prepared walker. In the most attractive regions, such as the National Nature Reserves or Forest Parks, footpaths are always clearly marked. More ambitious walkers often aim to complete the whole length of the long-distance West Highland Way, but it is possible to walk only sections of it. Remember that it is easy to get lost and that the weather can change rapidly at high altitudes. You can enquire about walks led by qualified guides at Visitor Centres and tourist offices.

Petrol

Out in the country, petrol stations are usually closed from Saturday lunch-time until Monday morning. If you are setting off into the far north at the weekend, make sure you have a full tank and, in remote areas, fill up whenever the opportunity arises, whatever the day of the week. The winding roads often prove to be much longer than they appear on the map and you don't want to get stranded!

ROAD ATLAS LEGEND

le Mans-Est	Autobahn mit Anschlußstelle	Motorway with junction
Datum, Date	Autobahn in Bau	Motorway under construction
Datum, Date	Autobahn in Planung	Motorway projected

® Raststätte mit Übernachtungsmöglichkeit
Roadside restaurant and hotel

® Raststätte ohne Übernachtungsmöglichkeit
Roadside restaurant

© Erfrischungsstelle, Kiosk
Snackbar, kiosk

Ⓣ Tankstelle
Filling-station

Autobahnähnliche Schnellstraße mit Anschlußstelle
Dual carriage-way with motorway characteristics with junction

Straße mit zwei getrennten Fahrbahnen
Dual carriage-way

Durchgangsstraße
Thoroughfare

Wichtige Hauptstraße
Important main road

Hauptstraße
Main road

Sonstige Straße
Other road

Bergbahn
Mountain railway

Sessellift (Auswahl)
Chair-lift (selection)

Autotransport per Bahn
Transport of cars by railway

Autofähre
Car ferry

Schiffahrtslinie
Shipping route

Landschaftlich besonders schöne Strecke
Route with beautiful scenery

Routes des Crêtes Touristenstraße
Tourist route

Straße gegen Gebühr befahrbar
Toll road

Straße für Kraftfahrzeuge gesperrt
Road closed to motor traffic

Zeitlich geregelter Verkehr
Temporal regulated traffic

—◄— 15% Bedeutende Steigungen
Important gradients

Kultur
Culture

★★ **PARIS**
★★ *la Alhambra*   Eine Reise wert
Worth a journey

★ **TRENTO**
★ *Comburg*   Lohnt eine Umweg
Worth a detour

Landschaft
Landscape

★★ **Rodos**
★★ *Fingal's cave*   Eine Reise wert
Worth a journey

★ **Korab**
★ *Jaskinia raj*   Lohnt einen Umweg
Worth a detour

※ ψ   Besonders schöner Ausblick
Important panoramic view

Nationalpark, Naturpark
National park, nature park

Sperrgebiet
Prohibited area

4807 ▲   Bergspitze mit Höhenangabe in Metern
Mountain summit with height in metres

(630)   Ortshöhe
Height above sea level

⌿   Kirche
Church

⌿   Kirchenruine
Church ruin

⌿   Kloster
Monastery

⌿   Klosterruine
Monastery ruin

⌿   Schloß, Burg
Palace, castle

⌿   Schloß-, Burgruine
Palace ruin, castle ruin

⌿   Denkmal
Monument

⌿   Wasserfall
Waterfall

⌒   Höhle
Cave

∴   Ruinenstätte
Ruins

·   Sonstiges Objekt
Other object

△   Jugendherberge
Youth hostel

Badestrand · Surfen
Bathing beach · Surfing

Tauchen · Fischen
Diving · Fishing

✈   Verkehrsflughafen
Airport

⊕   Flugplatz
Airfield

20 km
10mi

Distances in miles

Road Atlas of Scotland

*Please refer to back cover for an overview
of this road atlas*

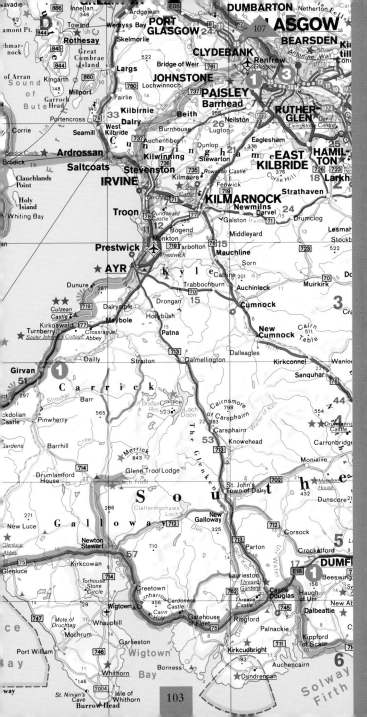

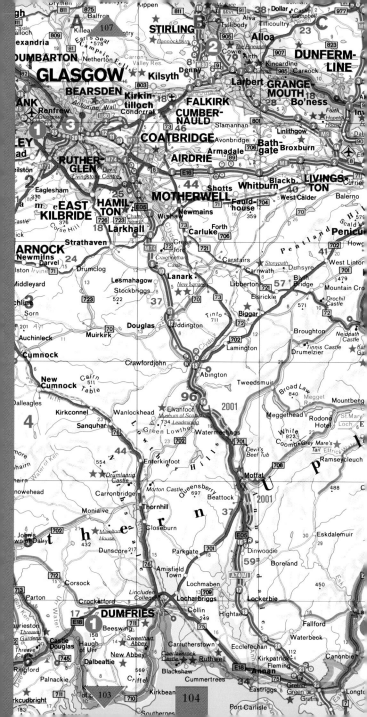

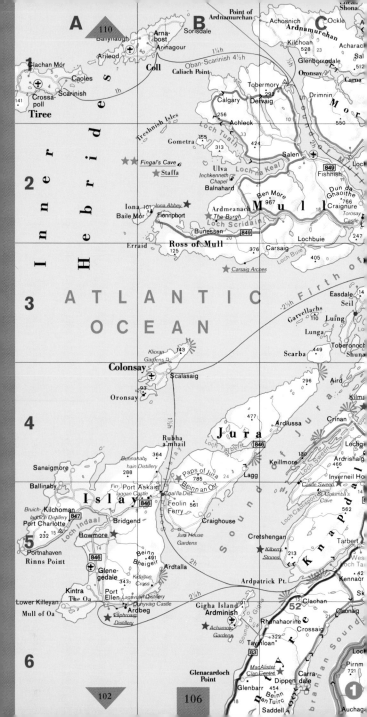

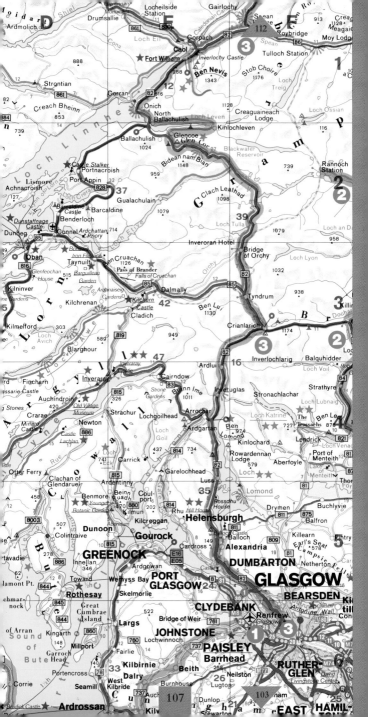

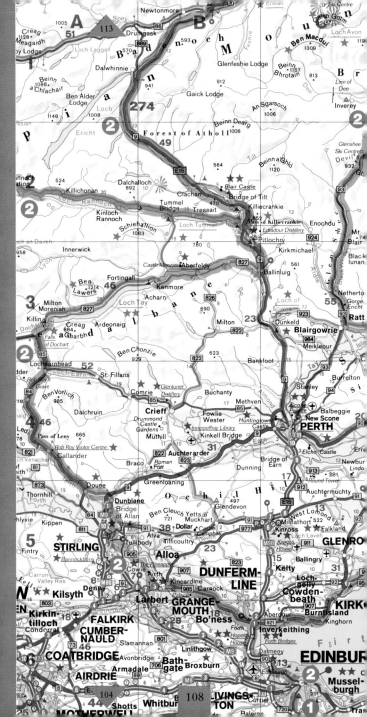

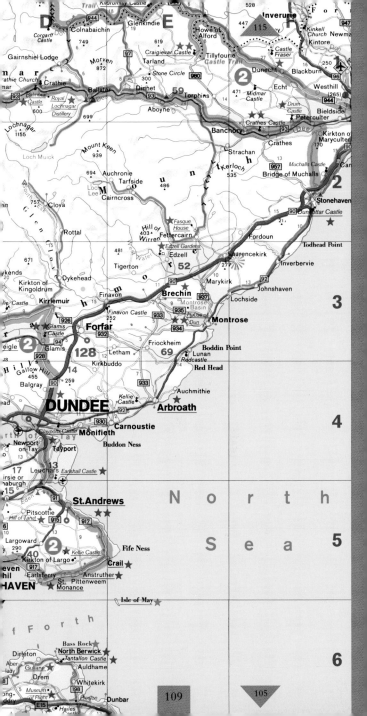

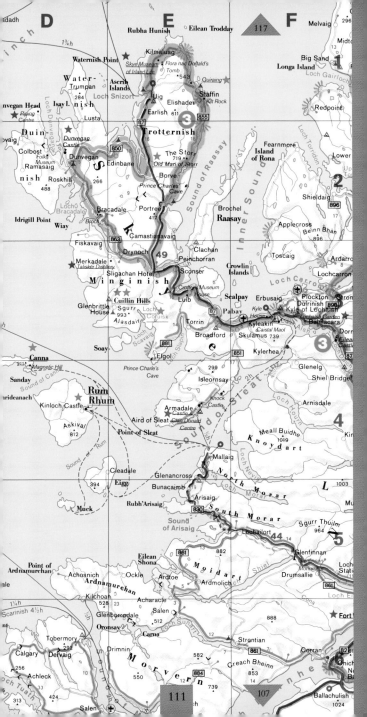

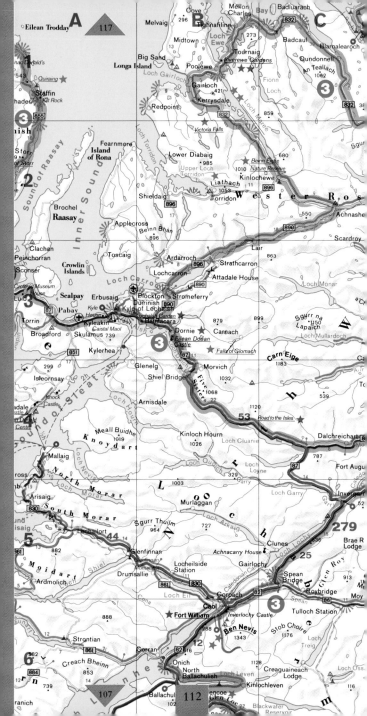

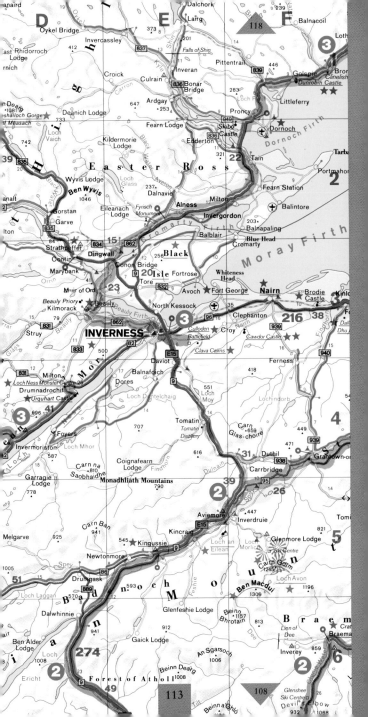

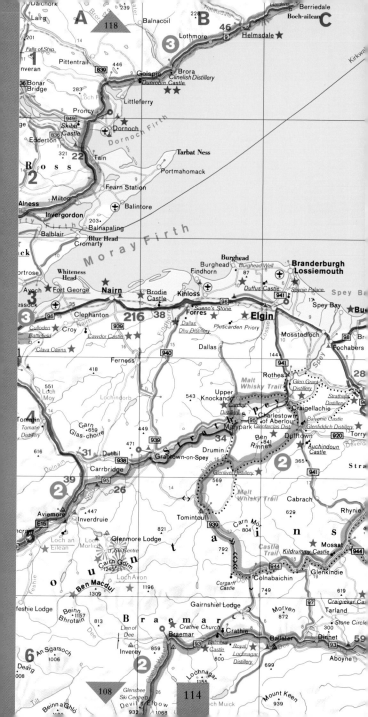

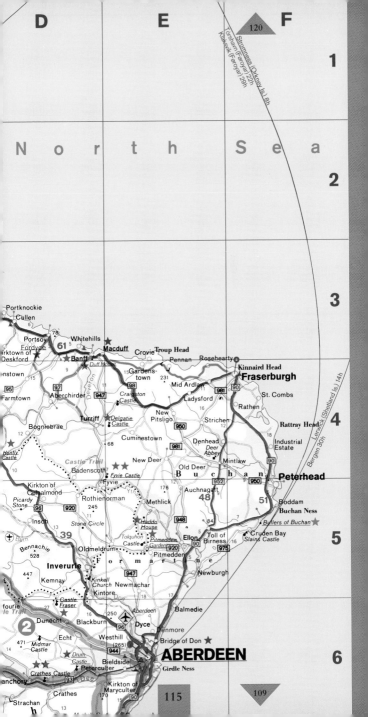

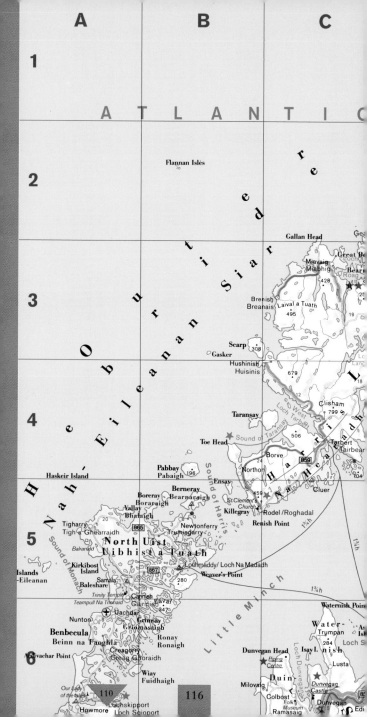

A B C

1

A T L A N T I C

2

Flannan Isles

Gallan Head

O u t e r   *H e b r i d e a n*   *S i a r*

Miavaig
Miabhig

Great Bi
Bear
Roag
MU
•428

25

3

Brenish
Breanais

Laival a Tuath
•495

19

Scarp
•308

Gasker

Hushinish
Huisinis

•679

Lc
Lan

N a h - E i l e a n a n   *S i a r*

H e b r i

12

18

Clisham
•799

L o c h   T a r b e r t

4

Taransay

Toe Head

Sound of Taransay

•506

Tarbert
Tairbear

Borve

Northon

•859

N a   *H e a r a d h*

Cluer

•04

Haskeir Island

Pabbay
Pabaigh
•196

Ensay

S o u n d   o f   H a r r i s

Boreray
Boraraigh

Berneray
Bearnaraigh

•459

St.Clement's
Church

Killegray

Rodel /Roghadal

Renish Point

1¾h

H a-

Tigharry
Tigh' a Ghearraidh

Vallay
Bhalaigh

•20

3

Newtonferry
Trumisgarry

865

5

North Uist
Uibhist a Tuath

Balranald

Kirkibost
Island

Samala
Baleshare

867

Lochmaddy/ Loch Na Madadh

Weaver's Point

1¾h

Islands
-Eileanan

S o u n d   o f   M o n a c h

•280

Trinity Temple
Teampull Na Trlohaid

Carinish
Cairinis

Eaval
•347

L i t t l e   M i n c h

Waternish Poin

Water-
Is

Nunton

Uachdar

Grimsay
Griomasaigh

Ronay
Ronaigh

Trympan
•284

Isay I. *n i s h*

Loch S

Benbecula
Beinn na Faoghla

Creagorry
Creag Ghoraidh

Dunvegan Head

Point
Centre

Lusta

D u i n

•Avachar Point

Wiay
Fuidhaigh

Milovaig

*Dunvegan
Castle*

Colbost

Folk
Museum
Ramasaig

Dunvegan

Edi

Our Lady
of the Isles

110

116

Howmore

Lochskipport
Loch Sgioport

1

O C E A N

2

Butt of Lewis
Rubha Robhannais

Church of St Moluag
Teampull Mholuidh   Port of Ness
[857]   Port Nis

The Trushel Stone   15

Shader
Lewis Black House   Siadar Iarach
[858]
Barvas
Barabhas   19

Garloway /Carlabhagh   248
Carloway Broch   12
  North Tolsta
  Tolastadh
Beinn Mholach   12   Tolsta Head
teasclete   291
  Upper Coll   Back /Bac
allanish   Laxdale   Col
[858]   .223 14   Broad Bay
Achmore   Lews Castle   Stornoway
Acha Mor   Steornabhagh
  St Columba's   Tiumpan Head
  Church   Portnaguran
Leurbost /Liurbost   [866]   Port Nan Giuran
Ballalan   Crossbost   Eye Peninsula
Baile Ailein   Crosbost   An Rubha
arvie   13

3

Kebock Head
Lemreway
Leumrabagh
Eilean
Iubhard

Sound of Shiant

3½h

4

Rubha Coigeach
Ach

Reiff

204

Shiant Islands
Nah-Eileannan Mora
Eilean an Tighe
  Summer
  Achiltibuie
  Isles
Priest Island   Tanera
  Mór

5

Rubha Réidh   Rubha Mór   Gruinard   Isl
  146   Mart
Cove   Mellon   Badluarach
Melvaig   296   Charles   Bay   [832]
  Tighnafilling
Midtown   Loch   273   Badcaul   Blarna
Hunish   Eilean Trodday   13   Ewe
  Inverewe Gardens   Tournaig   Dundonnell
ilmaluag   Big Sand   An Teallach
 um 1 /Flora nac Donald's   Longa Island   Poolewe   1062
  Tomb   .543   Loch Gairloch   Fionn
Quiraing   Loch
Uig   Gairloch   .421
Elishader   Kilt Rock   Kerrysdale   859
Earlish   611   Staffin   [855]
(3)   Redpoint   [832]
rotternish   Victoria Falls   (3)

The Storr
719
Old Man of Storr   Fearnmore   117   112
  Island   wer Diabaig
  of Rona   .985
  Upper Loch   Beinn Eighe   680
  1010   Nature Reserve

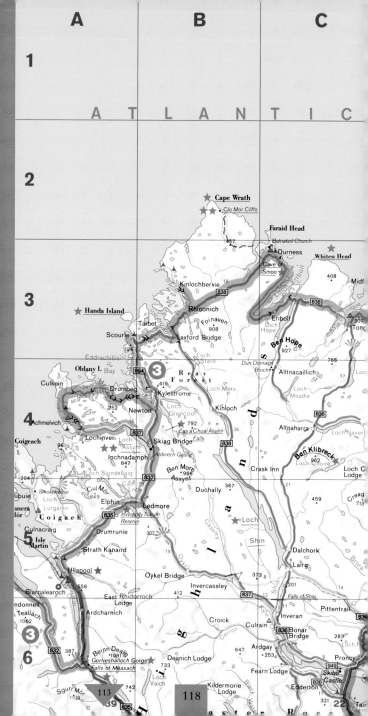

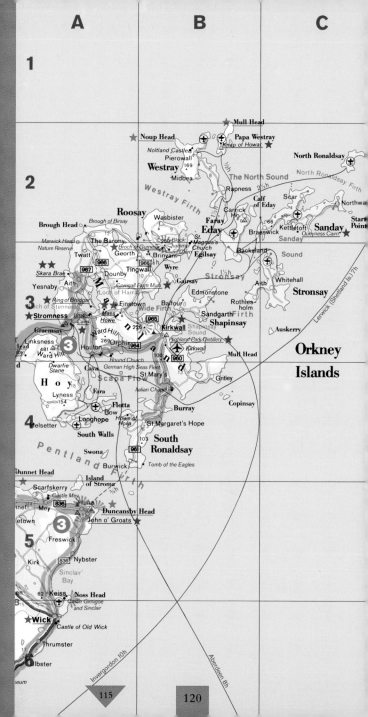

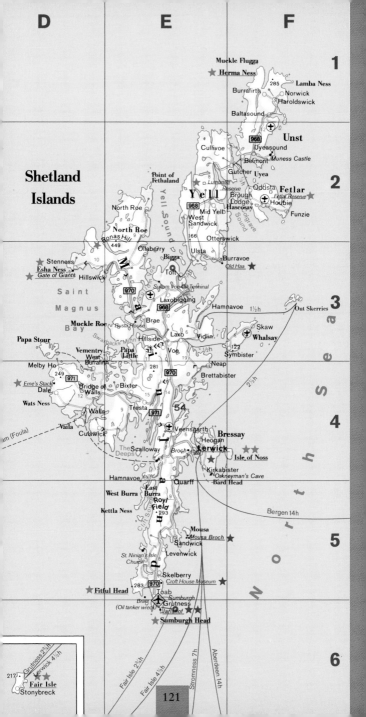

This index lists the main places and sights mentioned in this guide.
Numbers in bold indicate a main entry, italics a photograph.

122

INDEX

What do you get for your money?

 The pound sterling (£) is Scotland's unit of currency; one pound is divided into 100 pence (p). The bank note denominations are: £ 1, 5, 10, 20, and 50; coin denominations are 1, 2, 5, 10, 20 and 50 p, as well as £1. Scotland also issues its own bank notes, which are uniformly equivalent to the British pound.

Scotland has become a bit more expensive for tourists owing to the pound's recent increase in value. The average price for bed and breakfast accommodations lies between £12 and £18; in the larger cities, these prices increase by about a third. At the pubs, lunch costs between 3 and 5 pounds, a pint of beer is to be had for £1.60, and a whiskey costs between 96 pence and £1.15. Prices for a complete meal in a restaurant can vary between 7 and 30 pounds, although the normal range is £10-15.

If you are looking for somewhere more upmarket, then the sky's the limit and, in the cities especially, you will find a wide variety of good and reasonably priced restaurants to choose from.

Admission to municipal and state-owned museums and art galleries is usually free, although visitors are invited to make voluntary donations. Scotland's castles and stately homes are mainly run by the National Trust for Scotland (Tel. 0131 226 5922) or Historic Scotland (Tel. 0131 668 8600). Both of these organizations charge for admission, and prices can be quite steep, especially for families. They do, however, offer season tickets and week-long passes at discounted prices. There is an annual membership scheme which admits one person free to National Trust properties in Scotland, Wales and Northern Ireland. Write to the National Trust for Scotland Head Office, 5 Charlotte Square, Edinburgh EH2 4DU; Tel. 0131 226 5922. Admission to castles and country houses that are still privately owned costs around £6 per adult, children half price.

Petrol is cheaper in Scotland than in England. Car rental is also reasonable and rates are reduced from October to April.

£	US $	Can $
1	1.69	2.61
2	3.38	5.22
3	5.07	7.83
4	6.76	10.44
5	8.45	13.05
10	16.90	26.10
20	33.80	52.20
30	50.70	78.30
40	67.60	104.40
50	84.50	130.50
60	101.40	156.60
70	118.30	182.70
80	135.20	208.80
90	152.10	234.90
100	169.00	261.00
200	338.00	522.00
300	507.00	783.00
400	676.00	1044.00
500	845.00	1305.00
750	1267.50	1957.50
1000	1690.00	2610.00